The Cool Parents Guide to All of New York:

Excursions and Activities In and Around

Our City that Your Children Will Love and

You Won't Think Are Too Bad Either

* *

Alfred Gingold and Helen Rogan

* *

CITY & COMPANY * NEW YORK

This book is for Toby, cool kid par excellence.

Copyright © 1996 by Alfred Gingold and Helen Rogan

Maps copyright © 1996 by Al Pfeiffer

CITY & COMPANY

22 West 23rd Street

New York, NY 10010

Printed in the United States of America

Cover Illustration by J. D. King

Design by Leah Lococo

Library of Congress Cataloging-in Publication Data is available upon request.

ISBN 1-885492-35-9

First Edition

PUBLISHER'S NOTE: Neither City & Company nor the authors has any interest,
financial or personal, in the locations listed in this book. No fees were paid or ser-
vices rendered in exchange for inclusion in these pages. Please also note that every
effort was made to ensure that information regarding phone numbers, hours,
admission fees, and prices was accurate and up-to-date at the time of publication.
All phone numbers are area code 212 unless otherwise indicated.

Acknowledgements

Earnest thanks to Al Pfeiffer for his maps and suggestions; to Susie Bolotin, Cynthia Crossen, Becky Okrent, Barbara O'Neill, Katie Walters, and Sue Woodman for their words to the wise; to John Buskin and Betsy Carter for their generous cheerleading; and to Joan Arnold and Arthur Boehm for their shoe leather and companionship

—A. G. & H. R.

Table of Contents

Chapter One
Into the Melting Pot: Ethnic New York

Chapter Two
Museums: New Ways to Look at Old Things

Chapter Three
The City's Best-kept Secrets (Right Under Your Nose)

Chapter Four
Cityscapes: All Around the Town

Chapter Five
Action without Angst: You Can All Join In

Chapter Six
Pay for Play: Ten Treats that are Fun for Kids, Easy for Parents.   113

Chapter Seven
Downtime: Ten all-time great New York movies that you will be able to watch happily, at least for the first few times, with your kids.   119

Chapter Eight
Ten Places to Visit and Things to Do for Which No Parent Should Ever Be Too Cool.   125

What Is a Cool Parent?

A cool parent is one who does not view family activities intended for the child's enrichment as a vale of unrelenting boredom, typified by trips to diddly museums where some unemployed actress in a mobcap tells you about beeswax. No sirree. The cool parent has higher aspirations involving enjoyment, pleasure, *fun*.

Unfortunately, the cool parent in the quest for quality time doesn't get much help from newspapers and magazines. Children's listings tend to be arid, devoid of nitty-gritty: an address, a phone number, hours of operation, not much more. New Yorkers need to know more, and much more, before they set out toward parts unknown or even parts beyond their building. Sure, the Queens Museum sounds interesting, but how do you get there, and what do you aim for once inside? (Answer: a 40-minute subway ride from Times Square and the Panorama of the City of New York.) Is it easy to get from there to Stick to Your Ribs for barbecue? (It is.)

This book addresses the reality of being a (cool) New York City parent: discriminating, inquisitive, pressed for time, wanting to know there will be decent food nearby, and, above all, that children and parents alike will have a good time. Everybody knows how much there is to do in our city. What New York parents need is a little help finding the best of both the familiar and the offbeat.

To that end, *The Cool Parents Guide* offers a series of day trips, clusters of activities and sights, with enough variety and leeway within each of them to keep everybody happy. We tell you what to expect, where you can eat, and what else there is to see or do in the vicinity.

There are few children's museums in this book. Sure, they can be great for the kids, and you'll certainly visit your fair share of them before your parenting days are through; but no one in his or her right mind would claim children's museums are fun for adults. Likewise, we do not dwell on attractions that seem to us already well-known and utilized by New Yorkers, such as Central Park—which, if you haven't already visited, you really should. As devoted New Yorkers and parents ourselves, we guarantee all information for up to the minute (but not beyond) accuracy and attitude.

So all you really need to decide is whether or not you are cool. Read our manifesto and see if you match the profile.

The Cool Parents Manifesto

1. The cool parent demands the right, if only *in principle*, to enjoy family excursions, while acknowledging that this is not always possible (unless you're mad for cartoons or miniature golf). For some parents, coolness means never going to Disney-anything. So be it. (Although sometimes you do have to.)

2. The cool parent is mindful of the strategic importance of a cab, remembering the consequences of arriving at the appointed destination with kids already bored, exhausted, or whining.

3. To those who would persuade the cool parent to bring the whole gang to a mask-making workshop, we say: We'll get back to you.

4. Ditziness can be attractive in the young, but the cool parent always phones ahead for details, schedules, admission prices, and directions. The cool parent consults a detailed map *before* starting out. (That's why we've included some.) *Then the cool parent brings the map along!*

5. The cool parent always carries snacks, aware that kids have to eat when they have to eat and that gnawing hunger can mess up an outing before it's begun.

6. Speaking of food, the cool parent understands that there's more to family dining-out than McDonald's, Wendy's, and the local pizza joint.

7. The cool parent shuns like the plague parades, street fairs, food festivals, and the like for any child under the age of 10. Here's why:

* Little kids at these functions are routinely stepped on and elbowed.
* The noise and the crush is so great that you can't even hear what's wrong when your wailing child tugs at your arm and tries to tell you.
* Nothing could interest a child less than stained-glass doodads and foods of many lands.
* Brass bands, bagpipers, and steel drummers terrify them.

8. The cool parent is aware that at regular intervals the kids will need to "veg out," that is, to give up on meaningful activity and watch TV or do something equally moronic. Those inclined to guilt can make an enriching experience out of this, such as a Buster Keaton film festival with different kinds of homemade popcorn and other treats. You could even forget the homemade aspect.

9. The cool parent is an improvisational virtuoso. (By which we mean, if something isn't working, bag it.)

10. The cool parent knows that discretion is the better part of valor, and that, in New York, it always pays to keep your eyes open, especially in unfamiliar territory. But the cool parent is not a scaredy-cat, even when venturing into terra incognita (say, down a manhole in the middle of Atlantic Avenue, see page 57).

Is this you? Of course it is. As a New York City parent, you're already cooler than most, since New York City is the world's coolest place (and remember, our great city includes boroughs that are not Manhattan). We know that you're perennially up for the treasures, excitements, serendipities, and secrets that New York has to offer—except, of course, when it feels like a better day to stay home and lurk around, which is also a very cool thing to do.

How to Use This Book

Like Dr. Scholl's moleskin, these excursions should be trimmed to fit. Many of them include more than you and yours will be able to cover in one day. Our aim is not to exhaust you, but to provide frameworks within which you can create your own itineraries, depending on the ages, interests, and energy levels of your kids.

We live in a rapidly changing world, and nothing changes more often or arbitrarily than business hours. So we've simply provided all the necessary phone numbers. Trust no one but the horse's (or museum's) mouth. **CALL AHEAD FIRST**. (Another good reason to do so is to find out about additional programs and special events. Many of the institutions we recommend offer children's programs in everything from kite-flying to map-making. So go on, call.) All phone numbers listed in this book are area code 212 unless otherwise noted.

Subways are fast, and thus easier for children to ride than buses, so we provide subway directions, and bus routes only where essential. If you prefer to travel soley by bus, you can get all the information you need by calling 718-330-1234, a Transit Authority help line that is actually, of all things, helpful.

As of this writing, prices for the activities we recommend are moderate, by which we mean they are unlikely to cause more than the usual twitching as you reach for your wallet. When things get a little pricier—as in our Ten Treats (see page 113) for example—we tell you. But prices, as we all know too well, are subject to change; don't blame us if (when) they increase.

You are the best judge of whether your child is the proper age, gender, and type for the excursions we describe. So, with a few exceptions, we limit ourselves to telling you what there is to do and leave it to you to decide whether it's right for your family.

Chapter One

Into the Melting Pot:
Ethnic New York

A View of Old Manhattoes:
Inwood Hill Park with its Indian caves and intense baseball players, the Dyckman Farmhouse Museum, then lunch or a snack at Carrot Top Pastries.

At some point in their lives, Manhattanites—even the small ones— wonder what their island looked like before real estate developers started messing it up. The best surviving glimpse of that distant past is at Manhattan's northernmost tip, where **Inwood Hill Park** contains, among its nearly 200 acres, the largest natural woodlands on the island. Wear your climbing clothes for this one. Enter the park via Isham Park on Isham Avenue, passing the playing fields on your right; then bear to the right as the path diverges. Soon the foliage thickens, the walkway narrows and begins to climb, and the woods seem to loom: hickory, hackberry, yellow poplar, birch, sweetgum, spicebush (the twigs of which Native Americans used as chewing gum), and quaking aspen, whose leaves shimmer in the breeze.

Keep going until you see steep, rocky outcroppings up the hill on your left. The **caves** created by these overhanging ledges of rock were once inhabited by Indians. Time to leave the path; this climb is steep and requires some care, especially if the ground is wet. But it's not Everest, and in exchange for some huffing and puffing, you'll find deep, secluded niches in the rocks where the children can hunker down and you can remove yourself from the sights and sounds of the city. You may even see a shrew or vole—yes, this is true!— pleasantly rustic alternatives to New York's commoner rodents.

Once atop the cliffs, find the path that leads toward the Hudson River. The great view is even greater if you slip between the gaps in the chicken wire fencing on the path's river side.

When you come back down, pass the caves and go back down onto the original path. Continue along it until you come to a plaque where Peter Minuit's purchase of Manhattan Island from the Canarsie Indians was supposedly consummated. (In these leafy surroundings you can believe it, although those in the know say the deal was more likely closed at the Battery, where the Dutch had settled.)

Make sure to visit the brand-new **Urban Ecology Center**, operated by the Urban Park Rangers and housed in an old Columbia University boathouse. From here, you can go on guided nature walks and participate in various children's programs.

The best nature guide you could ever have had is a kindly, learned man named **Bill Greiner**. Bill claims he came here every day for the last 35 years; he certainly knows every path, plant, and stone. Equipped with a whistle and a stout walking stick, he led many a curious visitor to the caves or showed them where to gather nettles for soup. He led walks in Inwood Park over the spring and summer during which he cast a spell on children and their parents as he explained what the birds do, why the bark of a tree looks a certain way, and how come a path winds the way it does. Unfortunately, Bill no longer leads his tours, but the Urban Ecology Center has a calendar of events which offers something for everyone.

At the top end of the park you'll see the turbulent Spuyten Duyvil, where the Hudson and Harlem rivers meet, not amicably. You're at the tip of Manhattan island. Rowers in skulls glide by from the Columbia boathouse. And, weather permitting, some of the most **exciting baseball** to be seen in New York (recently, anyway) takes place on the diamonds up here. The teams are mostly Latin, and their game is skilled, hard hitting, and ferociously competitive. And you're right up close to it. Stand behind the batting cage, watching fastballs whiz by and waiting for the crack of ball on bat. It's a lot more thrilling than a game on TV.

Afterwards, head downtown to the **Dyckman Farmhouse Museum** on Broadway, Manhattan's only surviving

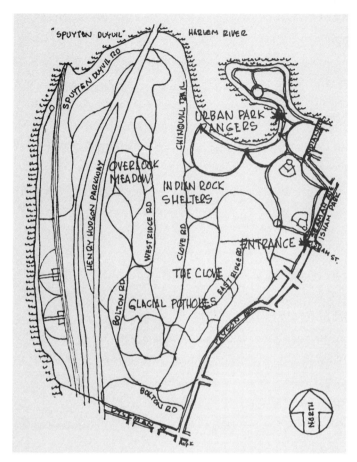

Dutch Colonial farmhouse. Built in 1784 and once the hub of a 450-acre spread, it has been painstakingly restored to its original condition and so it seems like a hallucination: a rustic antiquity on a completely urban street. Many of the objects on display belonged to the Dyckman family—though probably not the munitions, uniforms, and Hessian crockery you'll find in the Relic Room. The kitchen has great, sturdy cooking implements next to the open hearth. Right outside the kitchen window, scratched into the big stone outcropping, is a playing board for Nine Man Morris, an 18th-century children's game.

204th Street is bustling, so food isn't hard to find. Diagonally across the street from the Dyckman Farmhouse is a Dunkin' Donuts. But a few blocks up Broadway is **Carrot Top**

Pastries, owned by Renee Allen Mancino, whose renowned carrot cake has been called (in Molly O'Neill's *New York Cookbook*) the best in the world. This little pastry shop has a few tables and a small selection of sandwiches, quiches, and soups besides the home-baked goods (treat yourself to a hot apple pie as well). If you prefer, look for one of the many comfy Cuban-Chinese restaurants nearby, where children are welcome and can be made very happy with rice and beans, fried bananas, chicken and rice, and other not-too-spicy favorites. Remember, these Cuban-Chinese joints serve beer and wine, so pop a Corona and relax. The subway ride back home is always faster.

Inwood Hill Park (Isham Park entrance), Isham St. one block north of 207th St. and west of Broadway.)
Urban Ecology Center, 304-2365.
Call to receive a copy of their calendar of events.
Dyckman Farmhouse Museum, 4881 Broadway at 204th St. 304-9422
Carrot Top Pastries, 5025 Broadway at 214th St. 569-1532
Getting there: Subway: A train to 207th St. or 1 to 215th St.

* *

Downtown, Back When:
Sights of the old Lower East Side,
including the **Lower East Side Tenement Museum, Eldridge Street Synagogue,**
and various venerable shops; then uptown to the East Village, to **Little Rickie** and other hip emporia, ending with a casual meal at **Telephone** or **Two Boots.**

When the kids are old enough to be genuinely curious about the ways in which other people lived in other times, take a trip to the Lower East Side. You certainly do not have to be Jewish to be moved by what you can still see of its nineteenth-century immigrant past, particularly at the **Lower East Side Tenement Museum** on Orchard Street.

Buy your ticket at No. 90, and, while waiting for the tour of the tenement across the street at No. 97, make a point of studying the six-foot model of the "urban log cabin." It's like an immensely elaborate dollhouse but better, since it is filled not just with warming pans and four-poster beds, but also tiny representations of twelve families who lived in the actual tenement in 1870 (apartments on the right-hand side) and in 1915 (those on the left). They are shown in moments of their real-life dramas—languishing from tuberculosis, preparing for a seder, fighting with the landlord, sitting on the potty (the Shafer child, located in the third-floor rear, is a real crowd-pleaser). Written annotations keep you straight as to who's who. In a small adjoining room, screenings of assorted documentaries and oral histories fill in the picture of Lower East Side life earlier in this century and before. Best are the reminiscing old-timers. Their often heavily accented diction can be hard for children to understand, but the rhythms of the voices and the haunting photographs that come up on the screen will suck them in for a while, especially if you bribe them with the promise of a little something from the gift shop.

Across the street, a guide will lead you up the stoop and into a pitch-black hallway. The light (a twentieth-century addition) comes on and you're standing in a deep, narrow space with dark custard-colored walls, doors opening off it, and a steep staircase to the upstairs apartments. It's claustrophobic; it feels depressing and slumlike to a 1990s New Yorker, but the guide gently reminds you that when these places were first built in the 1830s, they were considered desirable. Two upstairs apartments have been painstakingly restored, and one room has been left as it was found—complete with layers of peeling wallpaper and old newspapers. In these rooms you can imagine the lives of Nathalia Gumpertz—a seamstress who, a century ago, supported her children alone after the inexplicable disappearance of her husband—and the Baldizzi family, Sicilian immigrants struggling through the Great Depression of the 1930s. All true, and all grist for a child's imagination.

After so much standing and listening, it's time to stroll. (Remember that on a Saturday almost all of the Jewish businesses down here will be closed.) Adults will linger at the venerable **Guss Pickles**, now located on Essex Street under an awning that says Essex Street Pickles. Big guys in Guss T-shirts preside behind the barrels, jovially ordering around their more timid customers and tolerating questions from tourists and others returning to check out their roots. Close by is the New Global Trading Company, where you can play gory Chinese video games in a pleasantly sleepy setting. Don't forget to peer into Rabbi M. Eizenbach's Religious Articles. One glance into its dim, cluttered interior—piled high with prayer shawls, books, and phylacteries—and you'll get the feeling that the rabbi has not inventoried his wares on a computer.

Now head off to the **Eldridge Street Synagogue**—in the 1880s, a sumptous place of stained glass and marbleized wood paneling; from the 1930s on, neglected; and now undergoing an elaborate restoration. (Opening hours are limited, so call first.) To continue in the faded glory mode, you could check in at **Streit's Matzos**, where the matzohs are made directly behind the sales counter, and take a short tour of **Shapiro's Winery**, where 30 different wines are fermented in cellars under the sidewalk, and enjoy a glass of rich, sweet wine (and grape juice for children) to top it off. Or else, walk to 290 Henry Street to see **St. Augustine's** Episcopal Church, built in the 1820s. You should have called ahead to ask if someone will be available to let you into the claustrophobic little "galleries," overlooking the nave, where slaves could worship while separated from the congregation. These reluctant immigrants were traded downtown at Pearl and Wall Streets.

The kids will be flagging by now, so you should do one of two things. Take them to **Ratner's**, the renowned dairy restaurant on Delancey Street, where the waiters are still rude and the onion rolls and blintzes are from heaven. Or walk uptown to check out the area's newest arrivals. Chinese, Ukrainian, and Yiddish slogans jostle each other on the storefronts, but as you look around you'll also notice intense young people in black who make their homes here now. This is the Area of the New Cool. While you won't be visiting any of the enticing-looking bars or artsy shops, you can stop in at **Little Rickie**, kitsch 'n' camp emporium par excellence. Want a light-up bust of Elvis? They have it, as well as wonderful tiny toys, postcards, lava lamps, puppets (the boxing nuns are much in demand), Mexican Day of the Dead paraphernalia, minute tea sets, paper dolls, scarabs, and games. It is heaven for all ages, and you can get out of there without spending a fortune, unlike some of the other adorable stores. **Love Saves the Day** has Davy Crockett hats and vintage lunch boxes at big prices; **Trash & Vaudeville** goes in for the six-inch tube skirts from England and magenta feather boas. Wherever you shop, the cost will mount up. Shrug it off and gloat over your purchases at a casual East Village restaurant like **Telephone Bar & Grill**, which has a jolly red English phone box a la Doctor Who outside as well as kid-pleasing bangers and mash or fish and chips inside. There's **Two Boots**, too, with its festive, tinsely decor, its combination Italian/Louisiana cooking (which actually works), and a patient and forgiving waitstaff that extends itself to make children feel at home. Sit down, cocktail in hand, and know that you've been good parents.

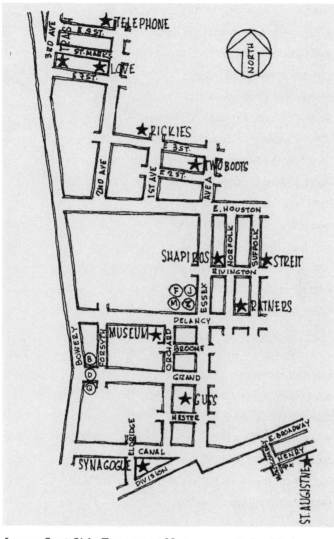

Lower East Side Tenement Museum, 90 Orchard St. bet.

Orchard and Broome Sts. 431-0233

Guss Pickles aka **Essex Street Pickles**,

35 Essex St. bet. Grand and Canal Sts. 254-4477

Eldridge Street Synagogue,

12 Eldridge St. just up from Division St. 219-0888

Streit's Matzos, 150 Rivington St.

bet. Essex and Norfolk Sts. 475-7000

Schapiro's Winery, 126 Rivington St.

bet. Essex and Norfolk Sts. 674-4404

St. Augustine's Church, 290 Henry St.

one block east of Chatham Sq.

Ratner's Dairy Restaurant, 138 Delancey St.

bet. Norfolk and Suffolk Sts. 677-5588

Little Rickie, 49½ First Ave at 3rd St. 505-6467

Love Saves the Day, 119 Second Ave. at 7th St. 228-3802

Trash & Vaudeville, 4 St. Marks Pl.

bet. Second and Third Aves. 982-3590

Telephone Bar & Grill, 149 Second Ave.

bet. 9th and 10th Sts. 529-5000

Two Boots, 37 Avenue A bet. 2nd and 3rd Sts. 505-2276

Getting there: F train to Delancey St.; B, D, Q

to Grand St.; J, M, or Z train to Essex St.

* *

Near the Narrows:
In and Around Bay Ridge, from the
Nellie Bly Amusement Park
to Fort Hamilton's Harbor Defense Museum,
taking time out for ice cream, parks,
and, of course, the Norwegian aspect,
with bakeries, delis, and even a parade.

A community of prosperous farms and luxury second homes long before it became a New York neighborhood, Bay Ridge has never entirely merged with the city. It's been home to many successive waves of immigrants (among the most recent arrivals are Syrians and Greeks), and you'll find evidence of disparate cultures wherever you look: Scandinavian bakeries, Italian delis, Irish pubs. Bay Ridge also has the greatest density of restaurants anywhere in New York aside, of course, from Manhattan. But for kids, the attractions are different; so different, in fact, that your first destination isn't even in Bay Ridge, but just west of it in Bensonhurst or Bensonhoist as the locals say.

Kids like amusement parks, but often their parents aren't amused. Coney Island can be too rough, though it needn't be (see page 86). The G-rated representatives of the genre, Great Adventure and Sesame Place, require hours of travel and pots of money. Fortunately, the discerning cool parent has an alternative: **Nellie Bly**, an amusement park you can be sure your small child will enjoy.

Nestled by the water, right off Shore Drive and just past Toys "R" Us, Nellie Bly is compact, a little shabby, and utterly benign. The rides are of the sweetly unthreatening variety—about the headiest are the bumper cars and the helter-skelter. Pretty much everything else is a variation on the carousel: planes in a circle, boats in a circle, motorcycles in a circle. The Fun House is nicely tame, although it does cough up the occasional weeping tot. Best of all, within an hour to 90 minutes, you'll have covered the whole thing, allowing you to return to a favorite ride or move on. The food is adequate and easy to find, as are the toilets. The result of all this? A good vibe, which you will see reflected in the people around you.

And what people! The families you'll see amount to a wonderful New York cross section. On a spring Sunday, you're likely to hear less English there than Yiddish, Russian, Chinese, Spanish, or Jamaican patois. Everybody's in a good mood, and there are many shared smiles of recognition as good-sport parents squeeze themselves onto tiny rides or cheer from the sidelines.

Afterwards, head for Fort Hamilton, a military base right at the foot of the Verrazano-Narrows Bridge that dates back to 1825. Here you'll find the small but fascinating **Harbor Defense Museum** housed in a little bunker called a caponier (French for "chicken coop"). It contains dioramas of naval battles, ship's models and antique weapons. Most impressive of all, it is on an actual military base; jeeps, cannons, and people in khaki are everywhere, guaranteed to keep children's heads swiveling. But beware: this museum is open only Monday to Friday, 11-4, and the same hours on the first Saturday of each month. It's closed on the first Monday of each month.

Next, head over to **Once Upon a Sundae** in Bay Ridge, a genuine old-fashioned ice cream parlor with a gleaming wooden counter, antique fittings, and several antique waitresses. This must be the only ice cream parlor in the city, if not the world, that isn't particularly child-friendly. Many of the regulars are blue-haired Bay Ridge ladies munching egg salad sandwiches, cups of soup, and little dishes of butter pecan, so decorum is expected. But you can oblige—for the sake of the homemade ice cream, which is so good that conversation dwindles away when it's served. If it's pizza you're after, try **Lento's** on Third Avenue, where the crusts are so thin and crisp the locals call the pies Eucharist pizza.

From here, visit the newly renovated **Owl's Head Park** at the northernmost edge of Bay Ridge. It's high, it has great playgrounds, and New York Harbor is spread out before you. Then take the footbridge over the Belt Parkway to **Shore Park**, the narrow ribbon of green that runs between the Parkway and the water. The sea breeze makes it a mecca for kiting enthusiasts. Fishermen, in-line skaters, and cyclists are out in force in all weather. And it was on one of these benches that John Travolta won Karen Lynn Gorney's heart, not to mention our own, in *Saturday Night Fever*. Don't even bother trying to explain it to Junior; you'll only embarrass yourself. If you've got the energy, you can walk a long way by the water,

right under the Verrazano-Narrows Bridge (look up for a glimpse of peregrine falcons nesting) and as far as Bensonhurst Park.

P.S. Every May, on a Sunday between confirmation and Mother's Day, Bay Ridge holds its annual **Norway Independence Day Parade**, the high point of which is the crowning of Miss Norway herself. (You'd think they would crown her in Oslo, wouldn't you?) There are the requisite vintage cars, hand-pumping pols, and several bagpipe societies of hefty Hibernians (sometimes referred to as "cops in kilts"), and more willowy blonde teenagers than you could ever have imagined living in Brooklyn and owning ethnic Scandinavian outfits. (In fact, they come from three states.) At **Nordic Delicacies**, pick up some venison meatballs and lingonberry jam. Real Danish pastries and a loaf of sweet limpa bread from **Leske's Danish Bakery** should tide you over on the endless trip home via the R train, the local of locals.

Nellie Bly Amusement Park, 1824 Shore Pkwy. 718-996-4002
Harbor Defense Museum, Fort Hamilton, Fort Hamilton Pkwy. at 101st St. 718-630-4349
Once Upon a Sundae, 7702 3rd Ave. bet. 77th and 78th Sts. 718-748-3412
Lento's Restaurant, 7003 3rd Ave. nr. Ovington St. 718-745-9197
Owl's Head Park, Shore Rd. at 68th St. and Colonial Rd;
Shore Park, enter from Owl's Head Park, via 69th St. footbridge over the Belt Pkwy., or, if you're going down the Belt by car, stop and park at any of the parking places.

Norway Independence Day Parade, from 92nd St.
up 5th Ave. to Leif Ericsson Park (at 67th St.); for details,
call Ruth Santoro at 718-836-3364

Nordic Delicacies, 6909 3rd Ave. nr. 69th St. 718-748-1874

Leske's Danish Bakery, 7612 5th Ave. nr. 76th St. 718-680-2323

Getting there: Bay Ridge is best reached by car,
but if you have no choice, take the R train to 77th , 86th,
or 95th Sts. and bring some hefty amusements for the young.
For Nellie Bly, take Exit 5 off the Shore Parkway.

* *

Chinatown's Familiar Exotica:
Strolling, shopping, and eating, with stops
at a *museum*, a *Buddhist temple*,
a *supermarket*, *toy stalls* that also sell
critters, an *arcade*, where you can play a game
with a talented *chicken*. Don't forget *lunch* (as if!)

Loud, bustling, and usually crowded, Chinatown can be an awful
tourist trap, but it's also an immigrant world with a proud history as
well as an invigorating present. Unfamiliar smells, sights, and
sounds are everywhere, a wall-to-wall bazaar of weird merchandise
and weirder food. Chinatown is eternally exotic to children; and
usually, they like Chinese food.

Start your visit with a painless history lesson. The newly renovated **Museum of Chinese in the Americas**
(formerly the Chinatown History Museum) on Mulberry St.
for a glimpse of Chinese-American life since the 1820s.
This small, kid-friendly museum
resembles a Chinese paper
lantern big enough to
enter. Inside are lots of
homely, evocative objects,

many of which can be handled: opera costumes, steamer trunks full of immigrants' possessions, kitchen utensils, musical instruments, shoes for bound feet, and clunky, eight-pound irons used by laundrymen.

After a look at what Chinatown once was, venture forth and see what it's like today. Stroll down Mulberry toward Chatham Square, the heart of Chinatown, then turn left and head up Mott, its main artery.

The pots of money said to be flowing in from Hong Kong have not, happily, diminished Chinatown's sublime tackiness, and nowhere is this more fully realized than at the **Chinatown Fair** at 8 Mott Street, home of the celebrated Dancing Chicken, who worked here for many years. Alas, she died, and no younger fowl has come forward to claim her tap shoes. But don't despair; the **Tic-Tac-Toe Playing Chicken** is doing very well, thank you. Her glass case seems a little tight, but the bird looks big, fluffy and healthy—and she can easily beat you at tic-tac-toe. The rest of the arcade is standard issue: loud games, close quarters, a general air of grime and unsuitability. Your children will love it.

Back on the street, you'll find yourself in tchotchke heaven. Everywhere there are laughing Buddhas, satin(ish) pincushions, ceremonial swords, velvet slippers, and tiny jade animals. Stay calm, though, and save some cash for the street vendors and newsstands where you can buy toys along with candy, newspapers, and hats. The most thrilling and different are the elaborate transformer samurai, each composed of smaller transformers. The figures tend to deconstruct when you play with them, but they look and feel great and the packaging has not one word of English on it, which greatly impresses the children.

You can buy tiny turtles in Chinatown, too; you see them piled in little dishes of water in shops and on the street. Be warned: It's illegal to sell turtles under four inches in length and all of these are. But if you have the urge to invest in this adorable contraband, it'll cost you as little as $3 or $4. Of course, that doesn't include the $100 or so worth of gear—tank, filter, light, heater—that you'll have to buy so your turtle lasts longer than a week. Still, the critter makes an excellent city pet, quiet, well-behaved and smaller than a *bichon frisé*.

If hunger pangs are beginning, stave them off with the eponymous, waffle-like specialty of the **Hong Kong Egg Cake Company**, a stall right off Mott on tiny Mosco Street. Or just feed your eyes; food is all around and much of the stuff you'll see for sale on the streets will be new to the children. Check out the fish markets for creepy-looking geoducks (enormous clams) and live blue crabs. The vegetable stalls brim with produce both familiar and alien. Look out for a large, fleshy melon called a durian—if it's been cut open, you'll smell it before you see it!

Meander the side streets. At **Jung Ku Books and Stationery** at 8 Pell Street, you'll find mah-jongg sets, handsomely illustrated calendars, and wonderfully illustrated flashcards for learning English, each drawing accompanied by appropriate English and Chinese words. (For a wider range of novelties, including Chinese checkers and lucky money envelopes, as well as books in English on martial arts and other subjects, try **Oriental Books and Stationery** at 29 East Broadway.) Step into one of the tiny herbalist shops that abound; your children's eyes will widen at the heaped ginseng roots, dried fungi, and ominous-looking potions on display.

By now, you may be ready for a quieter side of Chinatown. Among the Buddhist temples that dot the community, perhaps the most serene is the **Eastern States Buddhist Temple** on Mott Street, with incense burning and bronze

Buddhas gleaming in the candlelight. Senior citizens lounge in the anteroom, and there is a modest display of religious relics and statuary.

Finally the moment of truth arrives; where are you going to eat? Chinese restaurants and kids are a mutual admiration society; it's hard to go wrong down here. The new Hong Kong-style restaurants are better suited to children than dim sum parlors (fewer surprises). **New York Noodletown**, on the Bowery, is one such place; big, friendly, and bustling, it specializes in homemade guess what? Old-fashioned, Cantonese-style places are also excellent for families. Just south of Canal on Mott is the **Sweet 'n' Tart Cafe**, a small, tidy establishment whose menu, unusual even for Chinatown—includes gizzard, frog, intestine, along with dumplings, soups, and lo mein and, of all things, fresh fruit shakes. Or be adventurous and pick your own lunch spot. At the very worst, one of the kids will end up eating buns stuffed with duck feet.

Afterwards, stop into a local coffee shop (we like **Mee Lei Wah** on Bayard) for what look like enormous fried noodles dipped in honey. Or visit the **Chinatown Ice Cream Factory**, whose 36 flavors include almond cookie, green tea, and pineapple along with more familiar varieties. This shop also sells a bright yellow T-shirt depicting a dragon eating a cone; it's a winner.

Finish up with a souvenir for yourself at **Kam Man Food Products** on Canal Street, one of the largest markets in the area. Inside, it's less hectic than the street, and the range of merchandise is incredible. You'll find dried fish smaller than your finger, others longer than your leg, mushrooms of all sorts, innumerable varieties of soy sauce and other condiments, vast arrays of candy, cooking implements, and serving dishes. There's also a considerable array of Western candy and condiments. Why so much nougat and Bovril? It's because of the British colonization of Hong Kong—the English brought their food there and things like digestive biscuits were gradually assimilated into indigenous cuisine.

If you've got any energy left, and you're feeling international, stroll up to Little Italy. You'll find one of the best selections of tiny turtles and giant transformers en route at **Ning's** at 150 Mott. If you've got any room left after your lunch, stop in at the **Cafe Roma** on Broome Street. It has great cannoli and tortoni. Perched on spindly wrought-iron chairs, inspecting the day's purchases, you'll all feel deeply cosmopolitan, which is only fitting.

Museum of Chinese in the Americas,
70 Mulberry St. at Bayard St., 2nd fl. St. 619-4785
Chinatown Fair, 8 Mott St.
Hong Kong Egg Cake Company,
Corner of Mosco and Mott Sts.
Jung Ku Books and Stationery,
8 Pell St. bet. Mott st. and Bowery. 732-1030
Oriental Books and Stationery,
at 29 E. Broadway bet. Catherine and Market Sts.
962-3634
Eastern States Buddhist Temple of America,
64 Mott St. bet. Bayard and Canal Sts.
966-4753 (look in the window for the sign.)
New York Noodletown,
28 ¹⁄₂ Bowery at Bayard St.
349-0923
Sweet 'n' Tart Cafe,
76 Mott St. just south of Canal St.
224-8088
Mei Lai Wah Coffee Tea House,
64 Bayard St. 925-5435

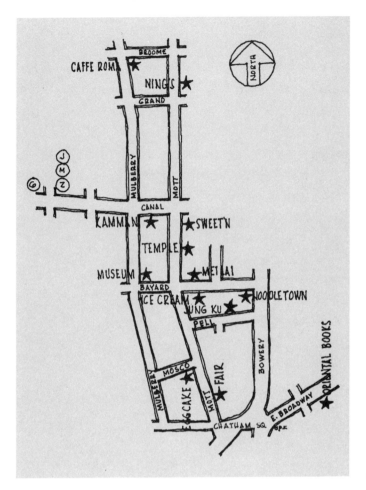

Chinatown Ice Cream Factory,

65 Bayard St. 608-4170

Kam Man Food Products,

200 Canal St. bet. Mulberry and Mott Sts.

962-8414

Ning's at 150 Mott St.

Cafe Roma Pastry,

385 Broome St. at. Mulberry St.

226-8413

Getting there: Take the F train to West Broadway

Chapter Two

Museums: New Ways
to Look at Old Things

Brooklyn's Best:
From the *Brooklyn Museum* to the
Botanic Garden, and *Grand Army Plaza,*
with time out at the *Greenmarket*
and *the heavenly luncheonette
that time forgot.*

If the **Brooklyn Museum** were somewhere else, it would be a premier attraction for tourists and local culture vultures alike. It has world-class collections (especially Egyptian, African, and Native American) and a building that looks the way a world-class museum is supposed to look—grand and looming. It has its own subway stop and a parking lot of respectable size—unlike that paved postage stamp in front of the American Museum of Natural History. And it's next door to the superb Brooklyn Botanic Garden. Even with all this going for it, the museum is rarely crowded. In short, it constitutes a great outing.

When you arrive, check your coats in the Grand Lobby, where there's always some extravagant installation, usually commissioned especially for the space. Your first stop might be the period rooms on the fourth floor; kids love to peek into furnished rooms of the past. Don't miss the ornate Victorian parlor, where a long double line of wooden animals winds across the floor to a Noah's Ark; the scene is watched over by the mysterious figure of a little girl with ringlets who sits, perpetually facing away from her twentieth-century visitors.

Next, the mummy in the Egyptian collection; it's real! And there's a wonderful gold ibis, which has become the museum's unofficial mascot. Then down to the ground floor with its towering totem poles, spooky masks, and New World artifacts. On your way to the bathrooms or the elevators, and always good for a giggle, there's Gaston Lachaise's voluptuous female nude. And there are two irresistibly well-stocked gift shops, one especially for kids.

When you get hungry, the light-filled, pretty cafeteria is on the first floor; the burgers are made to order and are pretty good. Or walk through the parking lot to the **Brooklyn Botanic Garden**, where there's good chili, sandwiches, and ice cream to be had while basking among the Conservatory greenhouses. Each of the four greenhouses is a different little world with its own climate—in the rain forest, the kids will get a kick out of the perpetual drips and the towering banana tree with its drooping load of fruit. In the desert, the motley array of cacti is stunning.

The Japanese Garden is not just serene and beautiful; it has turtles, ducks, and giant carp to feed (the ducks prefer whole wheat bread). Keep an eye peeled for the truly enormous turtle which, from time to time, ominously looms up out of the depths—the biggest critter in the pond by a wide margin. Stroll down the path by the pond. Head away from the Japanese Garden and soon you'll come to a steep, stone-lined alcove off to the side. While the smallest members fling themselves around this rocky redoubt, you can catch your breath and admire the scenery. If you're lucky, a heron will glide overhead to its nest in a tree by the pond.

When its thousands of species are blooming, the Rose Garden can make even the youngest jaw drop. Call for information about the Cherry Blossom Festival, which offers not just acres of blooms, but also Japanese music, dancing, and impressive martial arts demonstrations.

To return to Manhattan, turn left outside the main entrance of either museum or gardens and head for the subway at **Grand Army Plaza**, where—if it's Saturday or Wednesday—you can check out the **Greenmarket** for Ronnybrook chocolate milk, real Amish people, and the dour sheep farmers who, in addition to their lamb products, often bring wool and a working spinning wheel. On select days in spring or fall, if you're among the hardy few, you can climb the hundred or so steps to the top of the **Soldiers and Sailors Arch** for a spectacular view of Prospect Park, the harbor, and the city; or you can linger at ground level to watch newlyweds stepping out of white limos to be photographed in front of the fountains.

If you have time and appetites on your hands, head straight across Eastern Parkway and down Washington Avenue to **Tom's Restaurant**, an old-fashioned luncheonette festooned with artificial flowers and signs touting the cherry lime rickeys, egg creams, and banana-walnut pancakes. Everyone's friendly (especially owner Gus Vlahadas, who has been called "the friendliest man in Brooklyn"); the burgers are managable for small hands, the fries are crisp, and the egg salad not too mayonnaisey. It's not only the children who'll feel welcome.

Brooklyn Museum,
200 Eastern Pkwy. at Washington Ave. 718-638-5000
Brooklyn Botanic Garden,
1000 Washington Ave. 718-622-4433
Greenmarket at **Grand Army Plaza,**
Flatbush Ave. at Eastern Parkway
Soldiers and Sailors Arch at **Grand Army Plaza**
718-965-8968
Tom's Restaurant, 782 Washington Ave. at Sterling Pl. 718-636-9738
Getting there: On a sunny Saturday, take the 2 or 3 train to Eastern Pkwy (East Siders, take the 4 or 5 train to Nevins St., then walk across the platform). Get out at the Brooklyn Museum stop and you're there.

Queens of Arts (and Sciences):
An easy subway trip into *Flushing Meadows*,
Queens to see the *Unisphere*,
the *Panorama of the City of New York*,
the *Hall of Science*, and other delights.
Finally, epiphanies for all at *Stick to Your Ribs*.

Flushing Meadows in Queens has many delights, and you can explore them without the hassle of a car. You'll feel positively liberated to find yourself in such a wide and grassy space after stepping off the subway. And there are enough things to do, as you wander in and out of doors, for a couple of trips. If not, you'll have to choose.

Flushing is, of course, the place where two celebrated world's fairs were held. Checking out their remains has the thrill of an archaeological dig for adults, while the scale of the surviving structures alone will make the kids giddy and exultant. You won't be able to stop them from racing toward the gigantic *Unisphere* —which you've probably seen many times from the accursed L.I.E. (isn't it nice to be looking the other way?)—so follow along and prepare to be amazed. You are looking at the largest globe in the world. Made for the 1964 fair, the spherical grid with steel plates for continents is 140 feet high and weighs 700,000 pounds. In the summer, fountains play around it. Prepare for much frolicking on the steps around the pool; bring skateboards (it's a great, safe space) and the camera.

Another outdoor stop worth making is the *New York State Pavilion*, even though today it's a shell—big, round and empty. The floor is what you're here for: a decrepit mosaic of the whole state, complete with roads and town names. After the Unisphere, it's as if you're working your way down in scale, from the world to the state you live in. And for the next step down, head indoors.

The **Queens Museum of Art** is home to the **Panorama of the City of New York**, an architectural scale model of the whole city. It currently contains 895,000 tiny buildings as well as highways, bridges, and other landmarks. A couple of years ago it was renovated, and now you can walk around the edge of the whole area on a glass-bottomed ramp built a few feet above it. The room is subdued, with rapt people pointing and peering. At regular intervals a plane takes off from La Guardia, or the sky changes color and little lights gleam from within some of the houses as a Night Sequence unfolds. It's a heady experience, especially for kids—feeling big in New York City. (By the way, it's good to take binoculars; use them to focus in on your own, actual building.)

Just across Grand Central Parkway, and within easy walking distance, is the **New York Hall of Science.** Another wondrous 1964 relic, a building in the shape of a shimmering curtain, it's a welcome antidote for those burned out by New Jersey's Liberty Science Center. There's no glitz to bombard you; no big crowds to distract you. What's here is a low-key and peaceful hands-on museum which gives children umpteen scientific tricks to do. If they're old enough, they can learn from them; if they're really young, they'll have a great time just playing. There are giant bubbles and a 400-pound pendulum whose swing you can alter. You can make music on big pan pipes that pick up the ambient sound of the room; you can create optical illusions, mix colors, observe bacteria through a microscope, and power a fan as you pedal a bike. There's as much opportunity to move as there is to sit, and the friendly young staff are well able to pull a shy youngster into the swim. A renovation is due to be finished by April 1996, and this will include a revamped cafeteria and gift shop. There are good things to buy here—including a reasonably priced "starter" microscope (about $8); the inevitable astronaut ice cream is, and kids will concur, disgusting enough to put you right off space travel.

If anyone has the energy, the newly remodeled **Queens Wildlife Conservation Center**, just down the pathway is most appealing, with eleven acres of North American species and exotic birds soaring and perching right above their human visitors inside a Buckminster Fuller geodesic dome. And right next to it is an outdoor playground for all children—meaning that the equipment has been sensitively designed to also accommodate kids with special physical needs.

Hunger pangs are probably stirring just about now. And one of Queens's crowning glories is a restaurant, fifteen stops back on the No. 7 train toward Manhattan. **Stick to Your Ribs**, directly across the river from the Empire State Building, serves the best barbecue in New York. That's reason enough for some people to trek out to the cozy, steamy, red-and-white place with a Texas flag fluttering outside. For you, the key reason is that the kids will love it as much as you will. The atmosphere is down from casual—maybe "roadside" is a better term. There are a handful of formica tables, bright lights, great fragrant trays of meat brought in from the smokehouse outside, and blissed-out people eating smoky, savory barbecue off paper plates. There are also ribs, chicken, chopped pork on sweet Portuguese rolls, as well as outstanding homemade fries, beans, coleslaw, and a help-yourself fridge full of beer, soda, and brownies. And the staff are smiling, indulgent, and quietly amused at the rapturous expressions on the faces of the pilgrims eating themselves into satiety and beyond.

P.S. Stick to Your Ribs has opened an outpost on the Upper West Side, but the stuff isn't cooked on site. This one is the Real Deal.

Queens Museum of Art, New York City Building,
Flushing Meadows, Corona Park 718-592-9700

New York Hall of Science, 11th St and 48th Ave.,
Flushing Meadows, Corona Park 718-699-0005

Queens Wildlife Conservation Center,
Flushing Meadows, Corona Park 718-271-1500

Stick to Your Ribs, 5-16 51st Ave. west of Vernon Blvd.,
Long Island City 718-937-3030

Getting there: Take the 7 train from Times Square to Willets
Point/Shea Stadium. For Stick to Your Ribs, go back on the 7 to
Vernon-Jackson Aves. (the first stop in Queens) and walk two blocks
toward the river on 51st Ave. (the Empire State Building will be right
in front of you).

* *

Naval Engagement:
A day at the _Intrepid Sea Air_
Space Museum, topped off
with a meal at a zingy _fifties diner_
or the _Cupcake Cafe._

A trip to the **Intrepid**, way west on 46th Street, makes for a full-
size afternoon. The ships look daunting, and as you approach them,
you might be tempted to try the Circle Line Tour, which embarks
nearby. Resist—unless your kid is up for three hours on a boat listening to somebody talk—and take heart, this is a thrilling outing.

The museum is spread over six retired naval craft, ranging in size from an old harbor tug to the *Intrepid* itself, an immense aircraft carrier which served in World War II and Vietnam and was also, for a time, NASA's "prime recovery vessel." Begin your tour on the *Intrepid's* hangar deck. Ancient planes and battered space capsules dangle from the ceiling; the kids will make a beeline for the genuine fighter plane cockpit (it's hard to see how anyone larger than a child could sit in it, actually). Much of the space is given over to the *Intrepid's* role in World War II, with intricate table models of some of the ship's big engagements. They have the appeal of toys but are (fortunately) under glass. Your kids will be thrilled by the details—a Japanese airplane smaller than your finger tries to escape the great ship, but it trails a wispy cloud of cotton smoke, indicating it's been hit. Nearby, a bathosphere jockeys for attention with the "thrill simulator," a ride which rotates passengers upside down and sideways simultaneously. It may be how astronauts train, but not right after lunch. You can get a dog tag stamped for you while you wait on the hangar deck. They cost from $5 and up, depending on the metal (go for the plain Armed Forces Issue), and they're irresistible.

Find the plaque marking the spot where a kamikaze plane hit the ship, killing 30-odd crewmen. When you get to the words "You are standing on hallowed ground," the gravity of the place will touch you.

Clamber up onto the bridge—where weather-beaten, retired sailors will explain what all the buttons and switches do. Then wander below deck, where you'll find more intimate displays, tableaux of life-size mannequins in atmospheric settings. These are done with a real sense of theater. A group in one cramped room plots coordinates for the guns. Half-filled coffee cups, ashtrays, and moody lighting heighten the drama (and might frighten the smallest kids). The explanations accompanying these exhibits are unusually well written, especially those of the U2 spy plane scandal and the amazing capacity of helicopters to take off and land vertically.

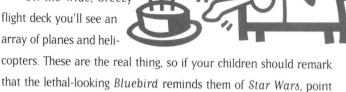

On the wide, breezy flight deck you'll see an array of planes and helicopters. These are the real thing, so if your children should remark that the lethal-looking *Bluebird* reminds them of *Star Wars*, point out that it is in fact the fastest plane in the world.

Before leaving the carrier, walk right to the end of the deck and look north. You can see the Little Red Lighthouse (a rare shore view) nestled under the New York pier of the George Washington Bridge (see page 42). And, if it's a weekend between April and October, you might see a cruise ship berthed next door at the Passenger Ship Terminals and readying for embarkation. You might even be able to smile at a load of departing pleasure-seekers in life jackets, gamely practicing a lifeboat drill.

If you're over six and you can fit through the small hatchway at its entrance, join the line to enter the nuclear sub *Prowler*. The sub is minute, suitably claustrophobic, and can only accommodate 17 reasonably lean and limber visitors at a time. The other boats are interesting enough and well-stocked with talkative old salts too, but if energies are flagging, head back east to Ninth Avenue, one of the city's great food bazaars.

Some lunch thoughts: On the way, you could stop at the **Market Diner** on Eleventh Avenue and 43rd Street a huge, old-fashioned diner, with everything on the menu from lobster tails to waffles. Over on Ninth Avenue, the cute and funky **Cupcake Cafe** is famous for its you-know-whats and also for its muffins, doughnuts, and cookies.

Take older kids for an early dinner at one of the dear old French restaurants **(Chez Napoleon** or **Tout Va Bien)** dating back to the days of the ocean liners. Go early before pre-theater rush sets in; see if anyone's up for snails.

Intrepid Sea Air Space Museum,
W. 46th St. and 12th Ave. 245-0072

Market Diner, 572 Eleventh Ave. at 43rd St. 695-0415

Cupcake Cafe, 522 Ninth Ave. at 39th St. 465-1530

Chez Napoleon, 365 W. 50th St. bet. Eighth and Ninth Aves.
265-6980

Tout va Bien, 311 W. 51st. St. bet. Eighth and Ninth Aves. 265-0190

Getting there: Even if you take the E train to 42nd Street,
you'll still have to walk four blocks north and four long blocks west.
The M50 bus stops right at the *Intrepid*, but if you're not in the
mood for a wait, take a cab west from wherever in midtown you
happen to be.

* *

Guggenheim vs. Whitney.
Into every young life some modern art must fall:
Choosing between museums—you know you've
got to take them, but to which one?

These grand Upper East Side institutions offer fine collections of modern art in small dosages, well suited for the young. Each trip makes an
interesting outing, with room for something else. But which will be
more rewarding? That is the question. And here are the answers:

Location, Location, Location
The Whitney's closer to the subway, but the Guggenheim's closer to
Central Park and to another short and sweet museum. **The**
Museum of the City of New York is only a few
short blocks away and has rooms full of extraordinary dollhouses
and antique toys.

Certainly, the Whitney's pretty close to the Park, too, but its
nearest neighbors, museum-wise, are the Met (too much for this
trip) and the Frick (under 16 not allowed).

Advantage: Guggenheim.

The Venue

While some question the Guggenheim's merits as an exhibition space, no one can deny that it's a great playground. For a start, more than one child has been known to compare the main tower to a gigantic toilet bowl; the giggles begin at that point. Inside, the space inspires action. Children race up and down the sloped floors and shout across the cavernous spiral. Be prepared for the art to be upstaged by stairway landings good for hiding. If you want your kids to look properly at the exhibits, don't start at the top of the ramp, which presents them with an irresistible downward slope. Instead, conduct your tour in a stately way, uphill.

The Whitney, on the other hand, is an interesting building if you like that sort of thing, but no one will ever mistake it for a toilet bowl. The single ticket booth and the solitary elevator (albeit a large one) create minor annoyances.

Advantage: Guggenheim again.

The Staff

The Guggenheim often teems with throngs of kids, and inevitably some of them run, shout, and, of course, try to touch the art, especially if the art is a big, soft, fabric slice of pie, which it might be. Perhaps that's why guards and clerks at the Guggenheim project a quality of having seen everything a museum guard can possibly see; nothing fazes them. As long as you *don't* touch the art, they are pleasant and helpful.

Whitney guards are cool and a little pushy, always realigning the omnipresent ticket queue. It must come from working on Madison Avenue.

Yet again, Guggenheim gets the nod.

The Food

The Guggenheim's cafeteria is small, but pleasantly decorated with the sort of swooping lines and curvy chairs you see on "The Jetsons." They serve modest cafeteria food at a modest museum markup.

The Whitney's food service consists of a sit-down cafe and a little snack stand with $5 sandwiches, coffees, snacks, and a few seats at a counter. There's usually a wait for the cafe.

Ho-hum. Where'd you rather eat?

Guggenheim again.

The Gift Shops

Both offer standard museum merchandise: lovely art books, prints, cards, ties, etc. and tasteful toys that won't get as much use as the price demands.

Draw.

The Art

By far the most important exhibit at the Guggenheim is Frank Lloyd Wright's. Beyond that, the Chagalls make an impact; they remind kids of dreams and fairy tales.

The Whitney's permanent collection includes Alexander Calder's *Circus*, which thrills children, and a very realistic sculpture of a leg sticking out of a wall with a candle growing out of its knee. Don't miss Charles Simonds' *Dwellings*, which looks like a miniature Pueblo village and sits on a ledge off the landing between the second and third floors, or Dennis Oppenheim's *Lecture #1*, a doll-size figure delivering an endless, soporific talk to row on row of miniature chairs. There are major works by such favorites as Hopper, O'Keeffe, and Warhol, but be warned: some of the works here are probably too graphic for children under 10 or so. Not so is another giggle-inducing Gaston Lachaise nude (see Brooklyn Museum, page 56) greeting you as you enter.

Advantage: Ours is not to evaluate the art of these museums, only to suggest that the Whitney makes it easy for a young person to focus on the art, so the Whitney wins this one.

Final Score: Guggenheim: 5, Whitney: 2.

Conclusion: Of course you'll go to both, but why not start with the Guggenheim? And if it goes horribly wrong, you're closer to the park than the toy stores.

The Solomon R. Guggenheim Museum,
1071 Fifth Ave. at 88th St. 423-3500
Museum of the City of New York,
Fifth Ave. at 103rd St. 534-1672
The Whitney Museum of American Art,
945 Madison Ave. at 75th St. 570-3676
Getting there: For the Guggenheim, the 4, 5, or 6 train to 86th St.; for the Whitney, the 6 train to 77th St.

* *

SoHo Art Trek:
An intriguing and accessible tour featuring
the *New York Earth Room*,
The New Museum of Contemporary Art,
and the *Guggenheim Museum SoHo*,
as well as nifty **buildings** to scope, **shopping**,
and **food** with transgenerational appeal.

There's more to SoHo than chic shopping and crowds. Start at the **New York Earth Room** on Wooster Street. The entrance is poorly labeled, and the stairs are rickety. But once you get to the top you're face-to-face with a permanent installation of crumbly brown earth, 280,000 pounds of it, piled to a level height of about 22 inches, spread across a white-walled loft space, and separated from you only by a Plexiglas partition that can be reached over. Not much going on here, only the occasional mushroom or weed poking its way up. What's so marvelous is simply the presence of the vast, brown living expanse; it almost seems to breathe. Some people become so attached to it that they come back again and again, and breathe along with it. (Note: the Earth Room is closed from June to September.)

Now head across Prince Street to Broadway (with maybe a stop at **Untitled** for postcards of every kind), and head north to two museums that are perfect for kids: **The New Museum of Contemporary Art** and **The Guggenheim Museum SoHo.** Both spaces are large and loft-like (the Guggenheim is on two floors) and they present eclectic and eye-catching work—neon, video, performance art, sculptures made of everything from beads to branches to silky-smooth marble.

Art creates a hearty appetite, which in this neighborhood can present a problem. People with older kids could head for **Spring Street Natural**, which offers varied, accessible vegetarian food in a cheerful setting or, in the other direction, the low-key **Cupping Room Cafe**, at West Broadway and Broome, for good pasta or hamburgers (the kitchen will produce small portions on request). Another good choice is **Bar 89** on Mercer Street, a hip, high-ceilinged, art-filled place; the bill of fare includes grilled cheese and burgers. If your children are in an unreceptive mode, consider the **Sabrett's** man who is usually to be found on the street just south of the Guggenheim. A hot dog eaten in the open air is one of New York's supreme delights, after all. If it's raining, or you need to sit down, there are two pizza restaurants on Broadway: **Piccola Pizza** and the funkier **New Tip-Top Pizza.**

After lunch, those with young children should drop in at **The Children's Museum of the Arts**, a veritable beehive of artistic activity. No looking here, just participation. There are floor-to-ceiling chalkboards, electronic sketch pads, activity areas with huge bouncy balls, and tables for painting, modeling, and making paper sculptures or mobiles; there's usually an artist presiding in some corner and, off to the side, a musician. This friendly, messy place clearly looms large in the lives of the local stroller set. Although there's enough here to interest kids up to 10, those in first grade and up will probably take one look at the clientele and slouch toward the door. Finally, stop in at **The Enchanted Forest** on Mercer Street, a quirky little toy shop tastefully decked out as a forest.

With older children, you can keep walking through SoHo, either crisscrossing your way downtown between Broadway and West Broadway or choosing the streets that are your favorites for **cast-iron architecture**—Greene Street has the most and the best-preserved. Broadway has three real beauties: the Singer Building (1904) at 561-563, the St. Nicholas Hotel at 521-523 (it was used as a Union Army headquarters during the Civil War— look up to see it at its best), and the Haughwout Building at 488-492 (the first building to use a steam safety elevator).

A choice of final stops—**Canal Jean** on Broadway, for the hip and fashion-conscious (great prices, wide and wild selection), or **Pearl Paint** on Canal Street, for your artsy kid. This is the preeminent craft store in the city, and it's not just aimed at children; so it's as well to know what you're looking for before you attack the five floors of beeswax, plaster of Paris, whittling tools, model kits, colored sand, and papier-mâché. When you come out of either store, laden with thrilling purchases, Chinatown (see page 28) will be beckoning. But you should save it for another day.

New York Earth Room, 141 Wooster St. 473-8072
Untitled, 159 Prince St. bet. W. Broadway and Thompson St. 982-2088

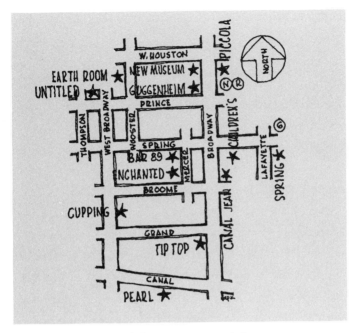

The New Museum of Contemporary Art,

583 Broadway bet. Prince and Spring Sts. 219-1222

The Guggenheim Museum SoHo,

575 Broadway at Prince St.; 423-3600

Spring Street Natural, 62 Spring St. at Lafayette St. 966-0290

Cupping Room Cafe,

359 W. Broadway bet. Broome and Grand Sts. 925-2898

Bar 89, Mercer St. bet. Spring and Broome Sts. 274-0989

Piccola Pizza, 594 Broadway bet. Prince and Houston 274-1818

New Tip-Top Pizza, Broadway at Grand St. 334-9790

The Children's Museum of the Arts, 72 Spring St.

bet. Broadway and Lafayette Sts. 274-0986 or 941-9198 for tape

The Enchanted Forest,

85 Mercer St. bet. Spring St. and Broadway 925-6677

Canal Jean Co., Inc., 504 Broadway bet. Spring and Broome Sts.

226-0737 or 226-1130 for tape

Pearl Paint Co. Inc.,

308 Canal St. bet. Broadway and Church St. 431-7932

Getting there: Take the N or R train to Prince St; C, E, or 6 train to Spring St.

* *

The *Metropolitan Museum of Art* x 2: A first foray and a second trip for your budding connoisseurs

Nothing Ventured, Nothing Gained.

For that first trip to the Met, stage a quick guerrilla raid, and then escape before the sheer size of the place becomes oppressive. Begin with the **Ancient Egyptian collection**; it never fails to enthrall, and it's right there on the ground floor. The children will look at the Temple of Dendur with eyes like saucers, particularly when you show them the photographs on the walls explaining the incredible engineering feat that brought it to New York. Also in the Egyptian galleries, are 23 Mekutra models, found in a tomb, each one illustrating a scene of everyday life, with tiny industrious clay people carting grain, rowing, and weaving. Of course, you have to find William, the Met's blue hippo mascot. Ask one of the dour guards for directions. Secondly, just down the hall from the Egyptian rooms, head for the massed **medieval armor**. The highlights of this exhibit are the armor-clad horses, the child's suit of armor, the assorted pistols, and the ferocious samurai warrior, in a suit made of steel and leather scales laced together with leather and silk. Here *awesome* is, for once, the appropriate word. And finally, in complete contrast, spend some time in the soothing space of the **Engelhard Court**, an indoor sculpture garden that features a Louis Comfort Tiffany fountain and loggia of extraordinary beauty.

P.S. The Met does a wonderful book for children called *Inside the Museum*, by Joy Richardson (published by the Metropolitan Museum of Art/Harry N. Abrams). Try to get a copy before you go, and the kids will be primed.

Second Try.

Capitalize on your previous success and go *upstairs* where you'll find Emanuel Gottlieb Leutze's **Washington Crossing the Delaware.** It is the largest painting in the museum, and the perfect place to start, because of its heroic scale and subject, and also because the artist committed three glaring historical inaccuracies. If they've all studied their copy of *Inside the Museum*, the kids will bring these mistakes to your attention with great zeal. While you're here, you can compare **George Washingtons** (Gilbert Stuart's portrait is here), and take in the Edward Hoppers and George Caleb Bingham's *Fur Traders Descending the Missouri* en route to the period rooms (building up to a Frank Lloyd Wright living room from a Minnesota house, a low-ceilinged, luxurious beauty, which can be viewed in the context of 300 years). Next, walk selectively through the European paintings. Don't even think of stopping before a Rubens, but you could certainly hold the children's interest with the perfect details of rustic life in **Brueghel's The Harvesters** and also—moving right along through the centuries—with the **Seurats** in all their dotty splendor. They're all here, van Gogh and Monet and Cézanne, but avert your eyes and head for surer territory, namely, the **twentieth-century wing**, which teems with big, bold, and witty paintings and structures that will immediately grab the attention of your budding connoisseurs. Next time, they'll be able to choose for themselves.

The Metropolitan Museum of Art,
1000 Fifth Ave. bet. 80th and 84th Sts. 535-7710
Getting there: 4, 5, or 6 train to 86th St.

Chapter Three

The City's Best-kept Secrets
(right under your nose)

Brooklyn Down Under:
A visit to *the world's oldest subway tunnel* and the *Transit Museum*, a dawdling stop over *homemade ice cream* and *Middle Eastern treats*, and, finally, the city's second-best view, from *the Promenade in the Heights.*

Brooklyn's oldest **subway tunnel** is also the world's oldest, and it's the singular passion of its (re)discoverer, Brooklyn native and railroad buff **Robert Diamond**, who conducts tours of his find when he feels like it. Make one of these tours the centerpiece of a day in, around, and under Brooklyn Heights.

Legends of Brooklyn's lost rail tunnel have existed for years. Robert Diamond heard them and set about finding the tunnel. After months of poring over ancient documents and newspapers and annoying city officials with his investigations, Diamond got permission to poke around underground. He went down a manhole at the intersection of Atlantic and Court, broke through a wall, and a 150-year-old breeze blew into his face.

That was 16 years ago. Since then, Mr. Diamond and a hard core of volunteers, the Brooklyn Historic Railway Association, have been slowly excavating the site. About a quarter mile of tunnel has been cleared. Mr. Diamond intends to keep digging right to the waterfront in Red Hook, where the track begins. He has more plans too, which he will enthusiastically share with you when he's not explaining tunnel-boring technology of the 1840s; why the developer who built the tunnel had it sealed not 25 years later; and why it was reopened in 1916, wired for electricity, then promptly shut.

Diamond's a spellbinding raconteur, and he has a few bloodcurdling anecdotes that will delight the children. (One unpopular foreman, for instance, was murdered and mixed into the mortar, so he is still, literally, on-site.) The entrance to the tunnel, down that manhole in the middle of Court and Atlantic, is a squeeze, and folks with claustrophobic leanings will feel a *frisson*. But the brick-lined tunnel itself, with its impressively high, arched ceiling, is stately and calming. The silence is total, with no hint of the traffic thundering above. Bring a flashlight and comfy shoes, and keep your eyes peeled for crickets, old nails and hardware, and nineteenth-century graffiti.

With subways on the brain, your next stop should be the **New York City Transit Museum**, which is housed in a now-defunct subway station two blocks away. It's a small place, but a civilized one. The exhibits of gears and turnstiles will intrigue the children, while the tokens, ads, maps, and Miss Subway tchotchkes will carry Proustian echoes for parents. Most evocative are the vintage subway cars that you can get into. Students of the native art of subway strap design will note a clear deterioration over the years; parents of a certain age may feel compelled to share memories of the straw-seated cars with bare light bulbs and chunky overhead fans. A documentary about the subway system runs continuously in the video room. The gift shop is excellent, a trove of postcards, pencils, T-shirts, Y-cut subway token jewelry, and train toys (even some *Thomas the Tank Engine* stuff).

Now back to Atlantic Avenue, for a restorative food stop. There are various possibilities: **Atlantic Bagel** for bagels and sandwiches; **Brawta**, a two-block walk down Atlantic and a bright, bustling, and wildly successful Caribbean restaurant (where you can easily find a non-spicy item for the kids); or **Peter's Ice Cream Cafe**, which, with its booths and ceiling fans, is an anomaly in among all the Middle Eastern restaurants and shops. The wondrous ice cream, cakes, and hot fudge are homemade. There are newspapers lying around. The coffee's good and doesn't come in alarming varieties.

Before leaving Atlantic Avenue, stop in at **Sahadi**, the Middle Eastern Zabar's (closed on Sundays), for Swiss chocolate bars, loose spices, fresh halvah, olives, dried fruit, pistachios by the bushel, and great hummus and keftah for supper at home—aaah! The aromas are great, and so are the prices. No credit cards, though. And of course you can't leave without investing in some flaky, sticky Middle Eastern pastries and cookies—stock up on them and on spinach pies at the **Damascus Bread & Pastry Shop**, a few doors down from Sahadi.

If you have the energy, just a few blocks away there's one great sight that's not to be missed. Walk through the leafy, narrow streets of the Heights to the **Promenade**: shake your fist at the skyline, or at least take in the extraordinary view of Manhattan (remembering that the true connoisseur favors the view from under the Brooklyn Bridge, see page 93). If the Promenade looks familiar even though you've never been there before, it's because every advertising spread in New York City seems to be shot there. If someone who looks like Norman Mailer jogs by, it's Norman Mailer; he's a local.

P.S. You can give any real train aficionados in your home a glimpse of the ornate and unused **City Hall subway station**, which is rented out to television and film producers. Take the East Side downtown local to the last stop. Remain in the

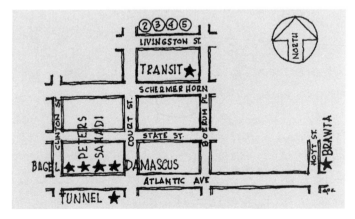

last car while it turns around for the uptown journey. Grab a glimpse of the station out the back window as the train pivots by.

Subway Tunnel, call the Historic Brooklyn Railroad Association to find out when Robert Diamond is leading his tunnel tour. 718-941-3160.

New York City Transit Museum,
Schermerhorn St. and Boerum Pl. 718-243-3060

Atlantic Bagel, 177 Atlantic Ave. bet. Clinton and Court Sts. 718-330-0303

Brawta, 347 Atlantic Ave. at Hoyt St. 718-855-5515

Peter's Ice Cream Cafe,
185 Atlantic Ave. bet. Clinton and Court Sts. 718-852-3835

Sahadi Importing Co. Inc.,
187 Atlantic Ave. bet. Clinton and Court Sts. 718-624-4550

Damascus Bread & Pastry Shop Ltd., 195 Atlantic Ave. bet. Clinton and Court Sts. 718-625-7070

Promenade, East River shore bet. Montague and Orange Sts.

Getting there: 2, 3, 4, or 5 train to Borough Hall. The tunnel tours begin outside the Independence Savings Bank on the southwest corner of Court St. and Atlantic Ave.

* *

In the shadow of the Great Gray Bridge:
Fort Washington Park
and the *Little Red Lighthouse*,
and, since you're up here, how could you
miss a chance to visit *The Cloisters?*

Unless you live in the neighborhood, just getting to **Fort Washington Park** is a challenge. But it's worth it. This little-known strip of green runs along the west shore of Manhattan, parallel to Washington Heights and right next to the water, from

158th Street to Dyckman Street. It offers great views of the river and the Palisades, woodsy trails, loads of sports facilities (during spring and summer the baseball diamonds are always in use, mostly by Little League teams, but the tennis courts are seldom fully occupied), and an ambience that's dreamy and tucked away.

And of course it's got the **Little Red Lighthouse**. Since it's not easily seen from our shores (or even from the George Washington Bridge), the lighthouse has assumed mythic status, as something everybody's heard of but no one's visited. However, it is undeniably there, tiny and red and nestled sweetly at water's edge right under the GWB, just as it says in Hildegarde Hoyt Swift's classic story *The Little Red Lighthouse and the Great Gray Bridge*. What a way to demonstrate to the little ones that sometimes it's impossible to tell if art is imitating life or vice versa! (If you don't know what we're talking about, go buy the book.)

The 75-year-old lighthouse stands on rocks, where once there stood a gibbet used to execute pirates. During spring and summer, it's occasionally open for the Urban Park Rangers' free walking tours, so call for the schedule.

Inside, the building is a small, empty cylinder, with a spiral staircase snaking up to the observation deck. A tiny parapet runs around the outside and you can walk on it, making sure to hold small hands firmly—the breezes are much brisker than you'd expect. Safely down, go and read the nearby plaque which celebrates the efforts of children all over the country to save the lighthouse when, in 1951, the Coast Guard planned to demolish it; apparently, the children's distress managed to soften even the stony heart of Robert Moses, who was Parks Commissioner at the time.

Be warned. There isn't anything in the way of an amenity here—no food concessions, no public bathrooms. But if you come up on **Little Red Lighthouse Day**, you'll find a bustling scene. This event takes place annually in the fall, and it has real local support. A stage is set up for bluegrass singers, story tellers, and sea-shanty types; Rangers stand good-naturedly around venerable boats once used on the Hudson; and earnest people at folding tables will hand you literature about ways to insure the future well-being of the Hudson.

The kids will love the Noc-Hockey and Ping-Pong tables, the horse-drawn-wagon rides, face-painting, barbecued hamburgers and locally caught bluefish—grilled and presented on toothpicks. An excellent T-shirt features the lighthouse on front and back. (Once home again, you'll feel you spent the afternoon at a country fair.)

Having come this far, treat yourself to **The Cloisters**, which is in Fort Tryon Park, only about 15 blocks north of here. (And if you haven't picnicked, the Fort Tryon Cafe has simple fare that will renew flagging spirits.) Once there, head directly for the Unicorn Tapestries. The drama and the mystery of this woven narrative crosses generations effortlessly. The knights' sarcophagi will prove to the children that there really were such people as knights. In the Treasury, seek out the illuminated manuscripts, and the sixteenth-century rosary bead carved from boxwood. The size of a walnut, it opens like a locket and has unfolding panels that form a triptych depicting scenes from the life of Christ. The detail is incredible, literally hundreds of minute figures are carved into this bead, complete with facial expressions, fingernails, and hair.

Next, stroll around the enclosed gardens, the cloisters themselves. The bare stone rooms and gloomy staircases right off the gardens are perfect for a quick round of fantasy play, because no matter how earnestly you explain what a cloistered monastery means, your kids will feel that this is a castle and act accordingly. If you all go stand on the parapet, with its brilliant views, you might think you're in a castle too.

Little Red Lighthouse, Fort Washington Park at 181st St. Call **Urban Park Rangers** at (800) 201-PARK to find out when the lighthouse is open and the day of the festival. They will also be happy to send you listings of all their free walks in whatever boroughs you request.

The Cloisters, Fort Tryon Park 923-3700

Getting there:

1. To the Little Red Lighthouse by car and foot: As of this writing, the 158th Street exit off the West Side Drive is closed. When it opens, it should still be possible to park in the packed-dirt parking lot that lies just south of Fort Washington Park. There are always cuchifrito stands here, as well as Dominicans barbecuing and playing merengue on their radios. It's a friendly family scene—a good place to start the long walk to the George Washington Bridge. Follow the river, and you'll get there. Alternatively, go north on the Drive to the bridge exit, then follow the signs to 178th Street. Turn left (under the bridge approach) when you can, go up to 181st Street and turn left again. Park as far west as you can. Walking west, you'll see the uptown leg of the Drive and a footbridge crossing it. Take the bridge and continue bearing left, downhill, toward the bridge.

2. To the lighthouse by subway: Take the A train to 181st Street and walk west until you see the uptown leg of the Drive. Then follow directions as above.

3. Going on to The Cloisters by car: Continuing from Fort Washington Park, drive north on the Henry Hudson Parkway. A sign will direct you to the museum's small parking lot.

4. Going on to The Cloisters by subway: Walk back along 181st

Street to the subway stop, then take the A train to 190th Street leave the station via the elevator and walk up through Fort Tryon Park.

P.S. The bus. If you've got the time and the temperament, substitute a leisurely bus ride for the subway home. The M4 bus goes from The Cloisters all the way down upper Broadway, crossing east on 110th Street and continuing down Fifth Avenue. Stare out the windows at the absorbing, changing cityscape before you.

* *

Three Cheers for Pooh! For Who? For Pooh:
A visit to the actual *Winnie-the-Pooh*
and friends with a side-trip to the
***Museum of Modern Art* and/or the**
Sony Wonder Technology Lab,
and *noodles* or *takeout* for sustenance.

Winnie-the-Pooh, the very name retains its hold over even the most determinedly current child. Take yours upstairs at the **Donnell Library** on 53rd Street to see the actual, original **Winnie-the-Pooh** toys that once belonged to A. A. Milne's son Christopher (aka Christopher Robin), and which inspired the illustrator E. H. Shepard. Seventy years old, dilapidated, and loved-to-death, the original Eeyore, Tigger, Piglet, Kanga, and, of course, the divine Pooh, still have soul. You'd recognize them anywhere; you'll want to take them home. People around the world have somehow learned that these animals are in New York; they make pilgrimages to see them and write heartfelt messages in the visitors' book. You will, too.

And now, you're right across the street from the **Museum of Modern Art.** Why not sneak in for a quickie visit? (Remember, children are much more relaxed about modern art than their parents are.) This is a very easy museum for them to like. Think expediently—it's much better to show them van Gogh than

Monet, pop art than photography. They'll love Lichtenstein, Oldenburg, Miró, Klee, Dubuffet—you name it. The design collections are great, too—furniture, appliances, and other thought-provoking but recognizable stuff from daily life. Afterwards, if the kids are behaving in a polite, European mode, head for the museum's cafe, or else go to a nearby noodle shop; **Dosanko** is only four short blocks south on Madison.

Or else you could do something very hip and different after Pooh. We're talking about a visit to the **Sony Wonder Technology Lab** in Sony Plaza on Madison Avenue, where children seven or eight and up can mess around on the cutting edge of communications by working some very fancy machines—and for free! The exhibit, located in Sony Plaza, is sleek and futuristic; courtly, skinny guys in black uniforms direct you to a glass elevator that zooms up four floors from the atrium and deposits you at the lab. Next, you have to log in, which you do by recording your name, image, and voice; then you use a little key card to get access to the machines. All this procedural stuff will deeply impress the kids, and this is before you've even really started! As for the machines, you can play recording engineer as you tinker with the mix for a music tape, see how medical imaging works, press many buttons to help solve an environmental crisis (oil spill, approaching hurricane), work robots, play video games, use sound and light special effects, and so on. It's all very clear and orderly; you just pick your machine, sit down, and log in. And at the end you get a graduation certificate with your name, picture, and list of accomplishments on it. This is an excellent place, but do try to pick a time when it's not teeming with school groups (they take precedence in the mornings, so you may have to wait on line for a little while). Afterwards, you can carry out a bite to eat from **Baked from Scratch** or **Cafe Society** (both of them right there in the atrium), which feature better-than-average sandwiches and salads as well as basic muffins, frozen yogurt, etc. And then you can all sit down to eat at a spindly little table in the bright, bustling atrium.

Donnell Library Center (Children's Room),
20 W. 53rd St. bet. 5th and 6th Aves. 621-0636
Museum of Modern Art,
11 W. 53rd St. bet. 5th and 6th Aves. 708-9400
Dosanko, 423 Madison Ave. bet. 48th and 49th Sts. 688-8575
Sony Wonder Technology Lab, Sony Plaza,
550 Madison Ave. bet. 55th and 56th Sts. 833-8100
Baked from Scratch, Sony Plaza,
550 Madison Ave. bet. 55th and 56th Sts. 421-6550
Cafe Society, Sony Plaza,
550 Madison Ave. bet. 55th and 56th Sts. 833-4089
Getting there: E or F train to Fifth Ave.

* *

In Between the Streets:
Move through Midtown, all the way from 42nd Street to 57th Street, the secret way—off-road.
And end up right outside Planet Hollywood.

New York adults love shortcuts known only to the cognoscenti; New York children love secret passages. Combine everybody's passions and impress your kids with this trip that takes you from West 42nd Street north to West 57th Street **without ever once using the avenues**. Make a trip of it (on a weekday, since some of the walkways are closed on the weekends), keep it in mind for a rainy day, and, most importantly, feel that warm glow that comes from knowing how to beat the system, even if it's only the grid system.

NOT£: Remember, unless you cross at the corner between each pass-through, you will be jaywalking. It goes without saying, only we're saying it anyway, that it pays to be very, very careful when crossing streets anywhere in midtown.

You could start by taking the subway passage from 42nd Street and Sixth Avenue up to 43rd Street, and cut through the Graduate Center of CUNY, but what you *should* do is use the stately lobby of 11 West 42nd Street, which cuts through to 43rd Street—20 West to be exact—and is altogether more elegant than the others. The vaulted ceilings, cut stonework, and touches of gold trim bring to mind the golden age of the Manhattan skyscraper; you feel as if you're in a Spencer Tracy movie.

Right across the street is 25 West 43rd Street, which emerges on 44th Street as No. 28. Another grand old office building, its lobby is as straight and narrow as the nave of a church; sharing the arcade with the elevators are old-fashioned stores—a barber, a tailor, and a shoe repair place. This building is the original home of the *New Yorker*; it looks it.

Across is 44th Street, No. 19-25 is the third and final of these statelys, The Berkeley, which becomes 18-25 West 45th Street. Unfortunately, there is no sister building across the street to shelter you. Instead, turn left and head west toward Sixth until you see a little pocket park that will take you through to 46th Street.

To continue your journey, cross Sixth Avenue and walk west on 46th Street, past the vast lobby of 1185 Sixth to the covered outdoor passage just next to the American Place Theatre. At 47th Street, you can enter the subway station and emerge unscathed three blocks north. But traveling via building can become habit-forming, so make for the covered walkway, at 133 West 47th Street. Once you hit 48th Street, you're in Rockefeller Center—you'll know by the increased incidence of carpeting, uplifting texts, and corporate art in the buildings. And by the proliferation of street vendors outside, selling terrific food to suit all tastes.

Go from 48th Street to 49th through the McGraw-Hill building at 1221 Sixth Avenue, then through 1251 Sixth Avenue (from 111 West 49th Street to 110 West 50th Street). Across the street you'll see the Time-Life Building, 1271 Sixth Avenue. Enter at 11 West 50th Street and, emerging at 51st, cross to the PaineWebber building. The inviting lobby here has a free art gallery, with some spectacular exhibits; but if you'd rather stay outside, go to 52nd Street via the Palio restaurant's pass-through. And now, for a four-star cool shortcut, enter Coopers & Lybrand at 135 West 52nd. You will meet a handsome wall of rosy wood—it's the elevator bank, and you can take a dog-leg turn through it and emerge at 53rd Street, just opposite the Hilton Hotel. It's easy to go through the Hilton, but more fun to take the passthrough west of it, particularly in warm weather, when you could stop for a bite at **Remi To Go**, a chic little outdoor cafe.

Between 54th and 55th streets, you have a choice of passages, one maintained by the Rihga Royal Hotel, another through the Ziegfeld Theater's parking garage, and a third beside the Ziegfeld; this is Fisher Park, with fountains, greenery, and places to sit.

On 55th Street, right next to City Center, you'll find No. 125, the offices of LeBoeuf, Lamb, Greene, and MacRae. The lobby here is open and security-guarded 24 hours a day and decorated with sculptures in the *Venus de Milo* genre. It's one of the few lobbies with an open-to-the-public policy clearly stated on the doors.

You emerge from Le Boeuf, Lamb directly across the street from the Parker Meridien Hotel, which maintains a pass-through alongside its lobby that is open daily from 7 a.m. to midnight. Closer to Seventh Avenue, you'll find the Carnegie Tower's Public Way, but the Meridien will deposit you only a few steps away from where the line forms for **Planet Hollywood**. Now, you may have been avoiding a visit here, but look at it this way: it's closer and cheaper than Disney World. The kids will adore the glitzy decor, the rambunctious rock music, the hamburgers-and-pizza food (which is decent), and the totemic movie memorabilia on display (E.T.'s phone, a piece of the Batmobile, and in person, Chewbacca). *Bon appétit.*

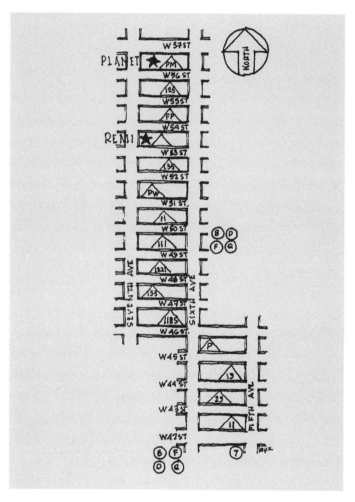

Remi To Go, 145 W. 53rd St. bet. Sixth and Seventh Aves. 581-7115
Planet Hollywood,
140 W. 57th St. bet. Sixth and Seventh Aves. 333-7827

Ah, Staten Island!:
Snug Harbor with its *Children's Museum,* the *Staten Island Zoo,* the *Alice Austen House,* and supper overlooking the Kill Van Kull.

Much of Staten Island is a best kept secret. In theory, therefore, you should use any excuse to ride the **Staten Island Ferry**. In practice, though, you might find yourself dawdling on arrival, since Staten Island public transportation, particularly on the weekends, is a sleepy affair. So, either go by car or bring something for the children to play with while you're waiting. You'll feel that you've left the city as you drive along quiet streets with frame houses, and tidy lawns, masses of utility wires overhead, and corner pizza parlors. Your focus will be either the **Snug Harbor Cultural Center** (which incorporates a children's museum) or the zoo. You could accomplish both, but then you'll miss out on the small town feeling of the island.

The **Snug Harbor** estate was built in the 1830s by a reformed pirate as a safe haven for retired mariners. He chose a site on a hill overlooking the waters of the Kill Van Kull, with a sweeping view of Manhattan. The buildings are a glorious mix of grand cream-colored Greek Revival buildings with colonnaded facades (these buildings contain dormitories, mess hall, meeting halls) and fairy tale-like dormered cottages where the staff lived. Much of this is open to the public, including the Newhouse Galley, with its jewel-like stained glass seascapes of lighthouses and ships.

Although the ghosts of the old salts still seem to roam the grounds, they have to share them with a cultural/artistic center. Large, inviting-looking sculptures dot the lawns and loom under the trees; the giant wooden grasshopper is excellent for climbing. Children love the spaciousness—80 acres with lawns, a duck pond, and serious Victorian gardens. But their special interest will be the **Children's Museum**, a small, hands-on, brightly colored place with a focus on bugs, as well as a number of artists' installations. These are distinctly kid-friendly, designed to have small persons walk through, touch, or peer into them. Even the smallest kids will be comfortable here, sloshing around in the water play area while their older siblings exclaim over the live, dead, and outsize grubs upstairs. Weather permitting, the gardens are great for picnicking. Failing that, check out Melville's Cafe, where they serve plain food—soups, sandwiches, bagels, hot dogs, and the like.

The **Staten Island Zoo** feels like a well-planned, small town zoo. Ride a pony, check out the porcupines, and feed the cows and ducks while hoping that the restless goats will stage a breakout (it happens). The surprising highlight is the reptile house. It's large, dim, and very well-stocked with turtles, snakes both vast and tiny, sharks and rays, iguanas and lizards, and of course fishes—loads of fishes. It's all on a scale that children are happy with—no lines, no jostling. Adequate snacks (taco chips, hot dogs, animal crackers, etc.) can be eaten at outside tables, and the gift shop is small and inviting.

While you're on the Island, don't miss another of its amazing views—this time, from the **Alice Austen House**, which is right on the water on Hylan Boulevard, across the street from a hideous high-rise. Originally a simple farmhouse, it was remodeled into a pastoral fantasy cottage by Alice Austen, the Victorian photographer who inherited it. The low-ceilinged downstairs rooms are shady and intimate, and on the walls are Austen's pictures of her family and friends at picnics and tennis parties, as well as haunting shots of the view, which has certainly changed over the course of a hundred years, as you will see when you step outside onto the lawns. They slope down gently to a rocky beach, littered with city debris that will prove fascinating to the younger members. Relax, you're more likely to find worn bottle glass, driftwood, and pieces of old foam or tubing than the dreaded medical waste. Up and down, right in front of you, pass the ships and tankers. To your immediate right (you certainly can't miss it) is the lofty sweep of the Verrazano-Narrows Bridge. Directly across is Brooklyn, and to your left, that inescapable Manhattan skyline. It's rare to find such a huge view in the city, rarer still to find it from the private grounds of a little white house with filigree decoration and a long Dutch roof.

You will be wilting by now, and there are a couple of McDonald's and pizza places around, but you don't have to do that. Instead, take Bay Street and then Richmond Terrace around the tip of the island and a little way past Snug Harbor. On the right, by the water, you will find **R. H. Tugs**; although it has enough wood panelling and Continental names on the menu to prompt subdued behavior in the youngest, Tugs will be more than happy to provide anybody who so desires plain pasta, a burger, a BLT or a big platter of French fries. The adult food is just fine. Meanwhile, the power stations and moorings of scenic Bayonne are on view just outside the big windows, as is the occasional monolithic container ship on its way up the Kill. As you eat, you can sense the workings of a still-busy harbor.

Snug Harbor Cultural Center,
1000 Richmond Terr. 718-448-2500
Staten Island Children's Museum, at Snug Harbor
718-273-2060
Staten Island Zoo, 614 Broadway 718-442-3101 or 3100 (tape)
Alice Austen House, 2 Hylan Blvd. at Edgewater St. 718-816-4506
R. H. Tugs, 1115 Richmond Terr. 718-447-6369
Getting there: For the Staten Island Ferry,
take the 1, 9, N, or R train to South Ferry and
follow the signs (call 718-815-BOAT for schedules).

By bus: For Snug Harbor, the S40 from the Staten Island Ferry; for the zoo, the S48 to Broadway, then walk three blocks; for the Alice Austen House, the S51 to Bay St./Hylan Blvd.; for R. H. Tugs, the S40, a few blocks from Snug Harbor.

By car: Verrazano-Narrows Bridge (lower level), to first exit on Bay St., for Snug Harbor and Alice Austen House. Clove Rd. exit for the zoo.

* *

Shhh, Voices Carry:
The Whispering Gallery at Grand Central Station
and other secrets of the terminal.

First, take in Grand Central Station's mighty Main Concourse, and gape up at the zodiac ceiling. It's hardly a best-kept secret, but the cleaning, which quietly commenced in 1995, is something you might not have heard about. Look at the portions of the ceiling that have been cleaned; you will be amazed at the turquoise color. Next, go down one level and stand under the glorious tiled ceiling just outside the **Oyster Bar**, where three corridors join. Position yourselves at the corners of the intersection, diagonally across from each other. Take turns speaking softly into the wall—the person across the way will hear every word you say. And then, if any of your party likes fish, go inside the restaurant. The golden room is irresistible, particularly if you sit at the counter, where you can take in the action. The fish is marvelous, and the desserts (apple pie, for instance) are traditional and satisfying. There are tiled vaults here, too, and the whispering gallery

effect they create means that you can hear people across the room more clearly than the person sitting next to you.

P.S. The **Municipal Arts Society** has a fascinating *free tour* of the station every Wednesday at 12:30. It's not designed for young children, but your preteen or teenager with a special interest in architecture or the history of New York would love it. Colorful factoids abound. Did you know that if you were to roll a ball down from the main entrance, it wouldn't stop until it reached the trains? The highlight of the tour is a walk across one of the "skybridges," narrow passages inside the huge, high windows that dominate the sides of the building. The public is not allowed in here; the scurrying figures in the concourse below don't even notice you, four floors above them, between two walls of glass. The sight spread before you is breathtaking. Afterwards, celebrate with a meal at the elegant little **Cafe at Grand Central**, which sits perfectly at the top of the Grand Staircase. As you eat chicken potpie or chili or sophisticated sandwiches, you'll probably be accompanied by the echoing sounds of a Peruvian band or a folksinger from the Music Under the Streets program, positioned below you, outside the Chemical Bank.

Grand Central Station, E. 42nd St. at Park Ave. 532-4900
Oyster Bar, Grand Central Station
(bet. Vanderbilt and Lexington Aves.), lower level 490-6650
Municipal Arts Society, 935-3960
Cafe at Grand Central, 883-0009
Getting there: 4, 5, 6, 7, or S train to Grand Central

Fabulous Festivals:
Unusual celebrations, from Native American Powwows to Tibetan Day on Staten Island, and *fresh ways to celebrate the old reliables,* such as *Independence Day* and *Christmas.*
These outings may be slightly removed from your natural habitat. But be bold and try them; they're winners.

Independence Night in Greenpoint

Bored on the Fourth of July? Try taking in the Macy's fireworks display. In Greenpoint. *Greenpoint?* Isn't that upstate? A savings bank? You want me to take my family to Greenpoint? Trust us when we say: You can do this.

Greenpoint (or *Greenpernt*, as it's spoken) is the northwestern tip of Brooklyn. It's full of Russians, Poles, and artsy types who've drifted over from Williamsburg and Long Island City. Its special secret: the piers, mementos of a bustling waterfront, which are *directly* across from the fireworks barge and much less crowded than the FDR Drive.

Not that you'll be in solitude. If you drive, leave plenty of time to park. Or take the subway; you'll get there faster and have a little time to stroll the streets. Besides, how often in your life do you get to take the G train? (You've heard of it, haven't you? Take the E or the F to Queens Plaza and transfer, or the L—the L!—to Metropolitan Avenue and transfer. Truly, you can *do* this.)

Stay on the G until Greenpoint Avenue. Walk east on Greenpoint (you won't be alone) until you dead-end on West Street. The piers are here; turn right and go up three or four blocks to the Huxley Envelope Company, 154 West Street. The pier to the immediate left of Huxley has the ideal mix of location, location, and location. The crowd is rowdier than Manhattan's but utterly benign; a lot of Russians and Poles are very happy to be here on July 4th and want to tell you about it. There are zillions of children and the view is almost as good as you'd get on television. But you're not watching television; you're in Greenpoint!

P.S. There's plenty of pizza and fast food around, as well as the Polska Restaurant, 136 Greenpoint Avenue, near Manhattan Avenue (718-389-8368), which serves huge helpings of homemade food from the old country in a clean and friendly setting. But by the time the fireworks are over, the hour and the generally overwhelming air of July 4th merrymaking make the best choice just gettin' home. After all, you've got a trip ahead of you; you're in Greenpoint.

Old Home Day at Historic Richmond Town, 441 Clarke Avenue, Staten Island 718-351-1611

This autumn extravaganza is held on the third Sunday in October at New York's answer to Williamsburg, Virginia, Staten Island's Historic Richmond Town. The village, a couple of dozen houses in various stages of restoration spread over what was once the provincial heart of Staten Island, is worth a visit at any time, but it's particularly jolly at this time of year. All the buildings are open, and friendly locals clad in period dress stroll the village streets, sit in front parlors, and demonstrate traditional crafts and trades. A gent in buckskins demonstrates the action on a muzzle-loading rifle he seems to have built by himself, or at least been heavily involved with. All the guides have a thorough knowledge of their subjects, from tinsmithing to soldiering and caning. Even if they are, in fact, struggling actors, they have real gravity and poise. You can buy hearth-prepared soup, bread, and sarsaparilla at the tavern, right near the roof-raising demo site. The Home Brewers of Staten Island are allowed to sell their root beer but not their more serious beverages, alas. They'll give you a little cup of beer, porter, or stout for free, though. A mesmerizing model train setup occupies most of the second floor of the Court House, whose vertiginous front steps are the staging area for bluegrass, harpsichord, and choir performances. There are free buggy rides and a great mound of hay for kids to jump into. As the light starts to fade, mosey down to the gristmill and watch it actually mill grist, then see if there are any ducks left on the pond behind. You're in New York City.

If you haven't filled up on Colonial soup, there are plenty of likely restaurants on Hylan Boulevard, the long commercial strip you'll travel to get home by car. (If you've chosen the ferry, the S74 is the bus you'll need.)

Tibetan Festival at the Jacques Marchais Museum of Tibetan Art,

338 Lighthouse Avenue, Staten Island 718-987-3500

The Tibetan Museum is a calm, secluded gallery, built in the style of a Tibetan mountain temple on the side of a steep hill overlooking terraced gardens, a lily pond with fish in it, and a distant view of Lower New York Bay. This little gem is open from April to November and we highly recommend it for anyone in need of an island of tranquility and willing to go to Staten Island for it.

But the time to take your kids is in the fall, for the Tibetan Festival. The mood is serene as ever, but there's also a blast of activity. Kids can cut out and color paper mandalas or yaks. There's an ancient-seeming, and artful, puppet show that you may, unbelievably enough, be able to bear watching with your children. Artisans and dealers sell Tibetan art (some quite gorgeous and expensive) and not-so-Tibetan wares in the garden, and your kids will actually enjoy some of the Tibetan food buffet (truly—the bread is soft and flat, something like a pita, and the vegetable dumplings are mild and savory). The one-room museum is dimly lit and atmospheric. It holds a three-tiered altar with gleaming figures in gold, silver, and bronze; many intricate carvings, a ceremonial apron made entirely of human bone; and a chart called the "Histomap of Religion: The Story of Man's Search for Spiritual Unity." Your little ones will be impressed, most of all with the monks—four rapt men in saffron robes who chant and ring little bells for hours on end. The spell they cast is palpable; whether you're a believer or not, a child or an adult, the sound is balm for the soul. (Just over four miles past Richmond Town, the Tibetan Museum can also be reached by the S74 bus from the Staten Island Ferry.)

The Christmas Lights of Bensonhurst

This comfortable, largely Italian neighborhood overlooks the Verrazano-Narrows Bridge and Gravesend Bay. Many of its homes are palaces, representing a wide range of architectural traditions, from antebellum Southern to Tudor to ranch. During the holiday season, houses here both large and small are tricked out in the most extravagant Christmas decorations seen outside of Rockefeller Center. Yards teem with light-encrusted trees, Nativity scenes, and life-sized Santas in sleds with reindeer in full flight. Flotillas of exuberant elves and masses of gingerbread men crowd each other right up to the property lines. The most elaborate decorations are on display from 79th to 86th Streets, between 11th and 13th Avenues. The indispensable block is 84th between 12th and 13th, where one home, called "Santa's House," features a row of elves making nutcrackers, Mrs. Claus rocking in her chair, and a smiling, waving Winnie-the-Pooh. Across the street is a colonnaded mansion in front of which toy soldiers 12 feet high slowly stride in unison, while around them life-size dancing figures cavort in peasant fustian. Over on 82nd Street, at No. 1054, Santa sits in the picture window, tickling the ivories of a grand piano. At 86th

Street and 12th Avenue, more massive wooden soldiers. By the end of your drive, you'll consider yourself lucky to be getting away with an adequately bedecked tree and the odd sprig of holly around the living room. Afterwards, take everybody out for some old-fashioned Italian food at L&B Spumoni Gardens, a family-style restaurant at 2725 86th Street (718-372-8400). P.S. A car is best for this, but you can take the B train to 79th Street or 18th Avenue. Bring trail mix.

The Dig-Your-Own Christmas Tree and Free-Range Reindeer Farm in New Jersey

A tree farm grows in Jersey, at **The Hazienda**, 101 Middletown Road, Holmdel, NJ (201-842-3309), to be precise. And the people who know about this place cheerfully put up with the hassle of a small trip for the sake of the beautiful trees and the chummy spirit that prevails here at holiday time. You can buy a pre-cut six- to eight-foot tree plus all manner of wreaths and trimmings; you can have one specially cut for you; or you can actually cut or dig your own (*bring tools*). There's more, in the chunky shape of Alaskan reindeer roaming free; a campfire for warming yourself; hot chocolate, French fries, and funnel cake to consume; a whole roasting pig (this could get mixed reviews from the kids); hayrides; and a nice, effficient staff to help and give you fresh apples upon leaving. To get there, take exit 114-N off the Garden State Parkway, and the entrance is 8/10 mile down the road.

P.S. You're on your own when it comes to tying your tree onto the roof of your car, so be ready.

Native American Powwows

Two or three times a year, representatives from tribes across the country (as well as Central and South America) gather somewhere in the metropolitan area to compete in dancing, chanting, and drumming; sell their craftwork; and raise public consciousness of their tribal identities. Powwows are great fun, especially the dancing. This begins after the drummers establish a groove and the chanters set up their hypnotic drone; men, women, and children circle, shuffle, and leap while the drummers begin to improvise, sitting in a huddle and taking their cues from each other. The sounds and the swirling feathers and buckskin are thrilling; children will realize immediately that this is the real thing. Don't miss the crafts, such as beaded belts, real (toy) spears or bows and arrows made of wood by real tribespeople. And try the food—everything from excellent buffalo burgers, chili, and Indian tacos to frybread sprinkled with powdered sugar. In 1996, the gatherings are in Park Slope, Battery Park, and Gateway Park, Brooklyn. Watch for advertisements or call the Manahatta Indian Arts Council, 718-499-5287; someone there will be delighted to give you information.

Clearwater's Great Hudson Revival

On Father's Day weekend, when you're looking for something special to do, take the car (or rent one) and drive up the Hudson to Clearwater's Great Hudson Revival, which takes place over two days. Started 19 years ago by folksinger Pete Seeger and dedicated to preserving the delicate ecosystem of the Hudson River, this lovely event is relaxed, old-timey, and welcoming. In 1996, the festival is being held in Valhalla, on the grounds of Westchester Community College. In previous years, it was held in Cold Spring, on the Hudson; and in the future, organizers are hoping to get to a riverside site once again. So call to find out. On several stages, many performers—some of the stature of Arlo Guthrie or Bonnie Raitt—will do their stuff. You can hear everything from zydeco or jazz to opera; you can sample ethnic foods and buy crafts. For the children, there's a special area with crafts and activities, a children's stage, and—at every turn—assorted storytellers, jugglers, clowns, magicians and mimes. Pete Seeger himself, that venerable sprite, may even be beaming from behind a microphone somewhere. So go, have fun, and do something to save our waters. Call 914-454-7673 for details.

Chapter Four

Cityscapes:
All Around the Town

You Must Take the N train:
(to Queens), where you'll find the
Isamu Noguchi Garden Museum
(for serenity), the *Socrates Sculpture Park*
(for art you can climb on), the *Museum of the*
Moving Image (for Mesozoic video games),
the *Omonia Cafe, Uncle George's, El Costal*
Columbia and more (for delectable food).

Two fascinating, highly specialized museums and one invigorating riverside sculpture park are all worth the short trip across the water to Queens.

If you're going by subway, take the N train to Broadway in Astoria, and walk west toward Vernon Boulevard and the East River. The dense commercial traffic gives way to residential streets and then warehouses. At Vernon, turn left and walk a block to 33rd Road. Look carefully up 33rd and you will see that the nondescript gray building which faces Vernon isn't so nondescript after all.

Sculptor **Isamu Noguchi** established his studio here in the 1960s in order to be close to the marble suppliers then operating along Vernon Boulevard. When he turned the place into a museum, he was careful not to disrupt the building's continuity with its surroundings. The result is probably the most hidden-away museum in the city, as well as the most serene.

Here you'll find over 350 works in stone, wood, and clay, including sculptures, lamps, and project models. The work, spare and abstract, is very accessible to children. The effects of the imposing stone pieces in the ground-floor studio often hinge on simple oppositions: hollow and filled, smooth and round, heavy and light.

In the garden, Noguchi interprets the traditional Japanese fountain, or *tsukubai*, is a massive stone cube from which water flows so quietly and smoothly that the stone seems sheathed in glass. Everything here is so tactile you'll want to reach out and handle it. Resist the temptation; touching is not permitted because, a guide explains, the natural oils in our hands are bad for the stone. Tell the children not to take umbrage—a very different museum is just a short walk away.

Return to Vernon Boulevard, turn right, walk two blocks or so north and you'll see **Socrates Sculpture Park**, almost five acres of not-at-all-manicured shorefront littered with a jumble of contemporary sculpture and set against views of the river, Roosevelt Island, and the Upper East Side. It is one of 14 "designated pedestrian sites" in New York and the city's most unusual picnic spot. Founded by sculptor Mark di Suvero in the 1980s as an informal gallery for local artists, the park has been bought by the city, which put up a plaque and, fortunately, left it at that.

The art here changes twice a year and its quality varies widely. But Socrates Park has a feature that lifts it above all competition for kids' interest: not one of the works on display here is off-limits. They can all be touched, sat on, ridden, rubbed, or run around. Indeed, many seem designed for hands-on use. As of this writing, your children can climb on an enormous green tree snake, run on a caged-in catwalk which surrounds four saplings, enter a steep brick amphitheater built inside a hill, or buddy up to a trio of larger-than-life teenagers on pedestals. Eat your picnic while relaxing in a nicely squishy-looking sofa made of mosaic tile.

Check out the fenced-off area diagonally across from the park's main entrance, the one that's patrolled by dogs (don't worry, it's a sturdy fence). With luck, you'll see sculptors in hard hats using cranes and other enormous contraptions to assemble some monumental work-in-progress. Elsewhere, young artists with their kids chat with friends and chisel marble between sips of coffee.

If it's not picnic weather, walk or take the Q104 bus back down

Broadway, and you'll soon be in the heart of New York's Greek-est neighborhood. Try **Uncle George's**, which looks like your standard coffee shop—except for the lamb roasting on a spit in the window and the more-esoteric-than-usual Greek specialties on the lengthy menu. Close by, but an ethnic world away, is **El Costal Colombia**, where you can get rice and beans, fried chicken, and other Latin specialties that small mouths enjoy. Where ever you go, save room for dessert and proceed to the **Omonia Cafe** on the corner of Broadway and 33rd Street. Here you can drink serious coffee and sample the rice pudding while the children put away lavish sundaes or gaudy, sticky cake—a favorite is the chocolate cake topped with an icing mouse.

Fortified, stagger another few blocks to the **American Museum of the Moving Image**, recently reopened after a renovation. The museum houses all manner of movie tchotchkes—set models and drawings, costumes, hair and makeup samples from *Planet of the Apes*, *Amadeus*, and the like, as well as exhibits explaining animation and special effects. In Tut's Movie Palace, a tiny (36 seats), riotously kitschy movie theater designed by Red Grooms, the kids can see classic serials from the golden age of film.

But for them, the absolute highlight will be the hands-on video game exhibit. They're all here: Donkey Kong, Pac-Man, and such cult classics as Star Wars, Karate Champ, Pole Position, and Space Invaders. Most are in working order and each has a card explaining its role in the saga of computer-operated entertainment. You'll use a lot of change, but save some for the gift shop. It's a good one: not just the usual logoed mugs and T-shirts and caps, but also posters, fridge magnets, claymation sets, and lunch bags of undeniable adorability.

Isamu Noguchi Garden Museum, 32-37 Vernon Blvd. Long Island City 718-204-7088 (Note: Museum is open only Wed., Sat., and Sun., from April to November.)

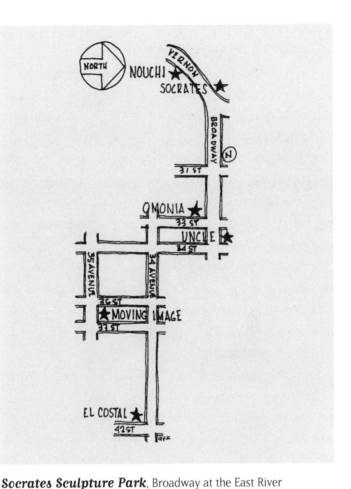

Socrates Sculpture Park, Broadway at the East River
American Museum of the Moving Image, 3601 35th Ave.
bet. 36th and 37th Sts., Astoria 718-784-0077
Uncle George's, Broadway at 34th St. 718-626-0593
El Costal Colombia, 34th Ave. at 42nd St. 718-706-0663
Omonia Cafe, Broadway at 33rd St. 718-274-6650
Getting there: For the Noguchi Museum, you can take
a shuttle bus from the Asia Society (725 Park Ave.) on weekends
(call 718-204-7088 for details), or proceed as described on p. 82.
If you opt for the car, take the Queensborough Bridge, lower
roadway, first right exit off bridge (Crescent St.) to 43rd Ave.
and then along Vernon Blvd. Parking around here is easy.

Brooklyn-by-the-Sea:

The *New York Aquarium,*
Coney Island, Nathan's fries . . . sigh,
Philip's Candy, Brighton Beach,
Mrs. Stahl's Knishes.

This is a big and busy trip, so prepare for a long day. Since the **Aquarium** draws a crowd year-round, it's best to get to this marvelous place situated right on the boardwalk early in the morning, when you can commune privately with the sharks without getting run over by countless little stroller wheels. There's a lot to see: the family of beluga whales (approach the windows quietly so as not to frighten the babies), endearing walruses, seals, otters, and penguins at the Sea Cliffs; exhibits of river and shore life, and giant rays, eels, and squid. Call to find out feeding times and special events. The food available for humans is adequate, but it would be much more fun to go right to **Coney Island**, just a few blocks west along the boardwalk.

The whole area is terminally decrepit and funky now, but the intermingled smells of fried food, suntan oil, and the sea are truly seductive, as is the mix of old-timers, young families out for the day, and expressionless hipsters all in black, smoking on the street corners. The police are discreet but ubiquitous, so you can feel safe. But make sure you're gone by sundown, when a less amiable mix arrives on the scene.

Coney Island's Astroland rides are thrilling for the younger set and safe enough for their parents' peace of mind. (But beware the deceptively tame-looking Tilt-A-Whirl. While your children are demanding their second and third turns, you might be parked on a nearby bench, head wedged miserably between your knees.) Bigger kids can brave whatever you will permit, from the Cyclone roller coaster to the Wonder Wheel or the enormous ship that swings sickeningly from side to side, high above the crowds. And you can look nostalgically around at the site of the former Dreamland and Steeplechase. Relics of the old days remain—the ruined Thunderbolt rollercoaster (complete with little cottage underneath, where the Timpano family lived, and which Woody Allen immortalized in *Annie Hall*) and the B&B Carousell (sic), almost hidden in a Russian flea market under the elevated train tracks across Surf Avenue. This carousel is tattier than others you'll find in the city (see carousels, p. 126), but unlike those, it still has brass rings to be hooked if you lean out far enough as you go whirling around.

Sometime in 1997, a much-missed Coney Island attraction by the name of Dick Zigun is due to return. Zigun used to run a truly peculiar boardwalk freak show called **Sideshows by the Seashore**, as well as the raucous and ebullient Mermaid Day Parade. He lost his lease, went out of business, and finally was rescued. And now, his whole gang—the swords-wallower, the tattoed man, the fire-eater, the snake-charmer, and all the rest of them—will be back in business in a big new museum-cum-theater space at West 12th Street and Surf Avenue. And with a cafe, no less!

Snacks are everywhere, of course—at **Nathan's** (good dogs, the world's best French fries) and on the boardwalk. There's even a McDonald's, if you must. Don't hesitate on the question of cotton candy—going home with a sticky chin is part of the deal. And right on Surf Avenue, just across from Nathan's and in the subway station is **Philip's Candy Store**, where a courtly man named John Dorman has been making and selling his chocolate, candy bars, jelly and caramel apples, peanut brittle, chocolate-covered bananas, and fudge to a devoted clientele for fifty years.

You're not going home yet. Instead, stroll back down to the boardwalk and along, sniffing the sea air, maybe going down to the sand to dip a toe in the water. End up at **Brighton Beach**, which is now an affluent Russian village. See how long it takes your children to notice that nobody around them is speaking English. Gape at the old-country delicacies, caviar and sturgeon, black bread and preserves. The prices are good if you want to stock up. See who can be the first to spot graffiti in Cyrillic script. And then, when everyone is truly starving, tackle a knish from **Mrs. Stahl's**, on Brighton Beach Avenue. They come in flavors—boy, do they ever! From cabbage to mushroom, by way of potato, kasha, apple and onion. Do not underestimate the ability of an adolescent to scarf these down. Buy in bulk and then slump contentedly on the subway all the way home.

New York Aquarium, Surf Ave. at W. 8th St. 718-265-3474
Sideshows by the Seashore, 1208 Surf Ave. at West 12th St.
Nathan's Famous Restaurant,
1310 Surf Ave. near Stillwell Ave. 718-946-2202
Philip's Candy Store,
1237 Surf Ave. in the subway station 718-372-8783
Mrs. Stahl's Knishes, 1001 Brighton Beach Ave.
at Coney Island Ave. 718-648-0210
Getting there: The D, F or Q train to W. 8th St./New York Aquarium at Coney Island. Return home by the D or Q from Brighton Beach.

* *

Where the Money Is:
Walking around _Wall Street_ and environs, with time for _the Exchange_, the _Criminal Courts_, art, history, and serious dinner.

This is a weekday tour and strictly for older kids. Start with the **_African graveyard_** on Reade Street just east of 290 Broadway. There's nothing there anymore except for a neat rectan-

gle of green lawn, planted with shrubs, set between the huge buildings. Nonetheless, its presence is haunting, especially when you read the sign stating that 20,000 or more Africans were buried there from 1629 until its closing in 1794. Continue east, to the forbidding **Criminal Courts** building on Centre Street. It's a sobering experience to tiptoe in and sit for a while, watching the endless procession of the (mostly) disadvantaged brought up before the judicial system. The bored policemen lounging against the walls, lawyers huddling and muttering, and the stiffly upright defendants—many of whom can't understand what's being said—are, for some, a sight right out of Dickens. For your children, it's a side of New York that they may know about in theory, but have probably never seen.

Now you're close to Wall Street. One of the most spectacular sights here has to be the bustling trading floor of the **New York Stock Exchange**, as seen from the visitor's gallery one floor above it. To be sure of getting a ticket for the short (30- to 45-minute) tour, show up before 11 a.m. (by 9, if it's a school holiday), since there will be a line for the limited number of tickets. The tour starts with a video and then, upstairs in the gallery, you can look down on the action as you listen to a taped description of what exactly all those intense-looking fellows in their colored jackets are doing. If your child has a real interest in the world's financial workings, you must book a tour of the **Federal Reserve**

Bank, just a few blocks away at the junction of Liberty and Wall. This place actually issues currency, and it houses more gold than Fort Knox, five floors of it, owned by the nations of the world. In the old days, international transactions used to be marked here by the transfer of gold; it was actually trundled from one area to another. They do let you see the gold, but there are two problems with the tour—you have to book a month in advance and you have to be 16. This will give it thrilling scarcity value to the average 16-year-old.

If you're starving by now, you're in luck. This area is fast-food central. Up and down the narrow little streets there are burger joints, pizzerias, etc. (It's worth just snacking now for the sake of an early dinner that's special.) Fortified, you can take an art breather outside. Start with **Louise Nevelson's Shadows and Flags** sculptural installation in the plaza right in front of the Federal Reserve. Look up from right in the middle of the seven jagged forms—they're designed to be viewed that way—and then cross the street, into the lower level of Chase Manhattan Plaza. You're facing a plate glass window, behind which is a characteristically discreet and meditative **Noguchi** work, a sunken garden with black rocks and lapping water. Walk past a striking car fender sculpture on the wall (*Triptych* by Jason Seeley) to the escalator, which will take you up to the outdoor plaza containing the wonderfully loony and idiosyncratic **Group of Four Trees by Dubuffet**. These looming black-and-white oddities, more mushroomy than tree-like, are a charming surprise here in the stuffy ambience of high finance.

Walk across Wall Street or Exchange Place to Broadway and check out the odd gorgeous lobby or architectural detail. You could walk down to the **Cunard Building** (now a post office) at 25 Broadway, for example, which has an incredible painted ceiling, as well as murals and frescoes, from the days when you could book your ticket on the *Lusitania* or the *Titanic*. And then walk up to the formidable **Trinity Church**, one of the city's richest institutions, rebuilt in its third incarnation to dominate Wall Street. (Literally—you can see it in front of you as you walk up Wall Street.) In the churchyard are buried Alexander Hamilton and Robert Fulton (the steamboat man). By the way, it was because Africans were not permitted to be buried here that the Reade Street burial ground came into being.

Look down Broadway to the Battery, and you get a sense of the small scale of old New York. Then walk west for the city's latest, slickest mode, exemplified by the World Trade Center, the World Financial Center, and Battery Park City, all built on some of the world's most expensive landfill. The **Commodities Exchange** is here, too, at 4 World Trade Center, and it's rawer and rougher than the Stock Exchange. These brokers are sweaty and shirtsleeved, and there's a lot of yelling. It's fun if you're not them. (Maybe it's fun for them, too.) The Commodities Exchange has been closed to the public "for security reasons" for a while and is due to open sometime in 1996.

Directly across the street is **Century 21**, the great discount department store where your Wall Street friends find incredible bargains on everything from toaster ovens to Calvin Klein undies. After a foray inside, you'll need a drink and a sit at one of the snazzy bars or eateries in the World Financial Center while planning dinner. **Odeon** on West Broadway remains the hands-down winner—it's enduringly cool, the young are welcomed (there's even a children's menu), and the food is as beguiling as the atmosphere. Reward yourself by ending with the crème brûlée.

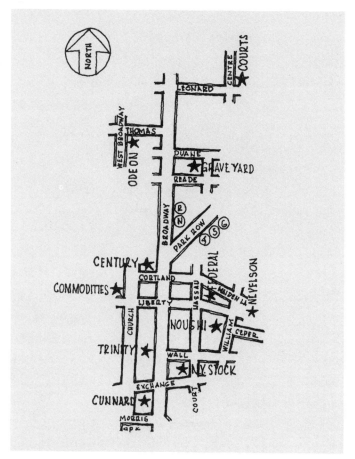

African Graveyard, Reade St., east of 290 Broadway

Criminal Courts, 100 Centre St. at Leonard St.

New York Stock Exchange, 20 Broad St. bet. Wall St.
and Exchange Pl. 656-5168

Federal Reserve Bank, 33 Liberty St. at Maiden Ln. 720-6130

Louise Nevelson Plaza, William and Liberty Sts.

Noguchi and **Dubuffet**, 1 Chase Manhattan Plaza at Cedar St.

Cunard Building, U.S. Post Office (Bowling Green),
25 Broadway bet. Beaver St. and Exchange Pl. 363-9460

Trinity Church, Broadway at Wall St. 602-0872

Commodities Exchange, 4 World Trade Center 748-1000

Century 21,

22 Cortlandt St. bet. Broadway and Church St. 227-9092

Odeon, 145 W. Broadway at Thomas St. 233-0507

Getting there: 4, 5, or 6 train to Brooklyn Bridge;

N or R train to City Hall

★ ★

Way Down South Street:
Empanadas for breakfast, a tour of the *Seaport*,
then over the *Brooklyn Bridge*
to *Empire State Park*, the *Fulton Landing*,
and world-class pizza at *Patsy's*

This trip requires energy and a lovely weekend day as you don't
want chilly gusts off the river to overpower the smallest member. So
fuel yourself up with a flaky, savory breakfast empanada at
Ruben's on Fulton Street. They have bacon-and-egg ones as
well as the more traditional spinach, or chicken. Start at the
South Street Seaport, which, despite its rampant commercialism and cranked-up Ye Olde Nautical aspect, turns out to be
invigorating and full of nice surprises. Don't bother to shepherd
your brood through the packed stores of Pier 17, which looks like a
mall anywhere. Stick to the old streets such as Cannon's Walk and
Schermerhorn Row, and soak up what's left of the nineteenth-century port ambience. (There are Federal-era buildings on Peck Slip,
between Water and Front streets, some slipping into decrepitude;
the oldest building at the Seaport is 273 Water Street, now a ruin
but formerly the house/store that retired sea-captain Joseph Rose
built for himself in 1773.)

To see everything, stop at the **Visitors Center** on
Fulton Street and buy a ticket that will admit you to two museums
(the kids' one is small, quiet, and interactive; your child might be so
charmed as to want to go through twice) and six historic ships. The

old sailing ships with their cramped living quarters and creaky timbers are haunting. You can also take in two short movies (the most exciting one features historic footage of the 1911 Peking fighting a storm), a couple of tours, visit the boat-building workshop, and whatever special event is going on—anything from Fire Day to the Festival of Maritime Work and Culture. (Call in advance to see what's on the docket.)

To recoup, buy a maritime treat from the cluttered, gimcracky little **Captain Hook's Marine Antiques and Seashells** gift shop—a nice hangover from the old days—then take a hot dog and an Italian ice to the riverside open space at Pier 15. Peer in at the boat builders on the corner of John Street or, at water's edge, check out the maritime crafts center where people work on model ships, scrimshaw, and figureheads. Alternatively, you could just hang out, watching the teenagers in billowing jeans show off their skateboard stunts for the tourists. Then head up to the **Brooklyn Bridge**. (Walk up Beekman Street to Park Row, turn right and you'll see the entrance to the walkway just across from City Hall.) It's magnificent up there, but scary, with the wind whistling through the cables and the maddened buzzing of the traffic below you. Hang on to the tinies, who should have a hat or scarf to protect their ears and sensibilities from the ever-present wind. And before going, bone up on David McCullough's *The Great Bridge*, so that you can give the kids a sense of the engineer's achievements and the odd gruesome details (20 involved in its construction, including its designer, John Roebling, died—most from the bends).

Coming down off the bridge (first exit to your left, left at the bottom of the stairs, and then left again), you'll find yourself on

Brooklyn's Fulton Street. Turn right, and walk down toward the river and the bridge. One of the city's most breathtaking and secret views is about to be yours. Turn right under the bridge approach, then take the first left down to the water. To your right is the **Empire State Park**, a little hilly meadow dotted with benches. On your left is a sweeping cobblestoned expanse that wraps around the anchorage of the bridge, and from it you can see past the Fulton Fish Market and the Seaport, past Wall Street's towers and canyons, past the Statue of Liberty and Governor's Island and out into the harbour. If you're lucky, a boat or two will sidle by; if not, the water will still lap at the pilings, and, chances are, you'll be uninterrupted in your skyline-gazing. (Although this is a quiet place, it's not dangerous. The River Cafe is next door, and there are artists living in the old warehouses up and down Front and Water streets; you see them relaxing in the odd neighborhood joint.)

And speaking of joints, the essential next stop is **Patsy's**, an old-style pizza parlor just up Old Fulton Street. You know the type: the owner is a dapper, white-haired gent; Frank Sinatra is on the walls and the jukebox, and the waiters are expert at swinging between the crowded tables without stepping on an errant 3-year-old. The fabulous pizza is slightly geared toward Mom and Dad—real mozzarella, fresh tomato sauce, delicate smoky crust; but rest assured, there is no goat cheese or radicchio to ruin it for the children. Patsy's is very popular, especially at kid-time (5:30 p.m. on) but the line moves fast, so stick with it. You will not regret it. And afterwards? Stroll down to the water again and the **Fulton Landing**, located just between Bargemusic and the River Cafe, the site of a ferry that from 1814 until the 1960s connected Lower Manhattan and the borough of Brooklyn. Now it has little benches and wrought-iron inscriptions from Walt Whitman, who lived close by. Then, flag down a taxi leaving the River Cafe, and go to the subway, or indulge yourselves and take it all the way home. Either way, the kids will fall asleep en route.

Ruben's Empanadas, 64 Fulton St. nr. the Seaport 962-5330
South Street Seaport Visitors Center, 12 Fulton St. 669-9400
Captain Hook's Marine Antiques and Seashells,
10 Fulton St. 344-2262
Patsy's Pizza, 19 Old Fulton St. bet. Water and Front Sts.
718-858-4300
Getting There: 2, 3, 4, or 5 train to Fulton St.; A or C train
to Broadway-Nassau. Walk east on Fulton St. to Water St.
Returning from Brooklyn: A train from High Street/Brooklyn Bridge

* *

Village People and Places:
the **Union Square Greenmarket,**
the **Forbes Magazine Galleries,**
Washington Square,
adorable little houses and streets,
Li-Lac chocolates (from heaven),
and a restaurant with a thing about cowgirls.

The Village can be hard for kids—too crowded, too much architecture and history, too many serious restaurants. This trip, preferably undertaken on a bustling Saturday, makes it fun. Start at the **Union Square Greenmarket** so that the children can fuel up with a little bottle of fancy juice and pretzels, muffins, or the chocolate chip cookies from Wilklow Farm, which, in addition to being large, also have the preferred ratio of chips to cookie.

Stroll down Broadway. If you're feeling expansive, stop in at **Forbidden Planet** and spend a few minutes amid the

pasty science-fiction fanatics while your children pick over the comics, figures, games, and posters. Then go west down 12th Street and across Fifth Avenue for the **Forbes Magazine Galleries.**

This place is a joy. Malcolm Forbes never put away childish things. On the contrary, he collected and cherished them, and much of his collection is on show here—12,000 toy soldiers, Fabergé eggs, presidential memorabilia, and more. The first gallery contains 500 toy ships and boats of all sizes and degrees of complexity, deployed in tableaux on gleaming glass seas. All around, you hear jolly nautical band music and the booming of ship's horns. The submarine display is the real kid-pleaser; the subs float murkily behind a long vertical window, you hear the ominous beeping of depth finders, and suddenly you notice a model of the *Lusitania,* sprawled on the bottom.

In the next gallery, there are toy soldiers and other figures, set up in tiny tableaux. You can see a pitched battle between Aztecs and Cortés's conquistadores, tiny wounded soldiers in field hospitals, Indians on a moving belt circling wagon trains, and regiment after regiment marching on parade. (Be warned: some of these tableaux are, incomprehensibly, too high up for children under the age of, say, 8. So you may have to hoist them up from time to time, or locate the stool that's usually somewhere around.) Don't miss the scene of William Tell preparing to shoot the apple from his son's head. Peer through a little porthole-shaped window in a room called Land of Counterpane, and you can pretend to be the child of Robert

Louis Stevenson's poem, with all your soldiers laid out in formation on the bed in front of you.

Two more stops include the presidential memorabilia for a look at Abraham Lincoln's actual stovepipe hat, the eyeglasses he dropped when he was shot, and his handwritten copy of the Gettysburg Address. Last, the Fabergé room, which, though it's more enthralling for adults, has aspects that children too will find fascinating—the miniaturization, the surprises—such as hens—tucked away inside the 12 gorgeous eggs made for the czars.

Next, go down Fifth Avenue to **Washington Square**. With luck, there'll be a pleasantly ramshackle assortment of buskers, magicians, and mimes—some of whom are talented (this is where Philippe Petit, the noted high-wire artist, used to perform). If your kids have a taste for the macabre, point out the ancient Hanging Elm at the northwest corner of the park, once used for public hangings but, sadly, since 1992, missing the relevant branch.

Now for the most Villagey aspect of the tour. Walk west two blocks, to Seventh, preferably along **Bleecker Street**. Here, in among the tourist traps, there still are rundown record stores, bakeries, and lovely old cafes with tin ceilings. West of Sixth Avenue, you'll hit the enticing Italian food shops; you owe it to yourselves to invest in bread from **Zito's.** At Seventh Avenue, turn south, and head for some of **New York's oldest, prettiest blocks**. Of course they look familiar; you've seen them in countless movies. Take a right, down St. Luke's Place to Hudson Street, then up Morton Street, then left again into Bedford Street. Here you'll find No. 75 $\frac{1}{2}$, a house which is not merely New York's narrowest (at 9 $\frac{1}{2}$ ft.), but which was also inhabited by Edna St. Vincent Millay, John Barrymore, and Cary Grant—in that order. Walk west down Commerce Street to the Cherry Lane Theater. Commerce dead-ends at Barrow Street; turn right, back toward Seventh, cross Bedford, and you'll see on your left a mysterious little stone courtyard. Walk in. Ahead of you is a forbidding, heavy barred door with no sign—swing it open and you'll find yourself in **Chumley's**, once a speakeasy and now a convivial bar with framed book jackets on the walls, a world-class jukebox (rivaled only by that in the Corner Bistro on West 4th Street), and a roaring log fire. Children are allowed to eat here; the food is eclectic and fine. But if you have more energy, go out the back entrance onto Bedford (another door without a sign), and turn right until you hit Grove Street. At the corner, gape awhile at Twin Peaks, a truly eccentric house at 102 Bedford, and at the tiny frame cottage in front of it. Then make a left and keep walking until you see another secret place—Grove Court, a perfect row of six small red houses dating from 1854, tucked away in their private courtyard.

Surfeited on architecture, the children need rewards. Take them to **Li-Lac**, the old-fashioned French chocolate shop on Christopher Street, where you can dither happily over the selection of chocolates handmade in the back room, and then think about dinner. Obviously there are masses of places to choose from—the Elephant and Castle on Greenwich Ave. at 11th Street, John's Pizzeria on Bleecker, and any number of taquerias and cafes. But, for a change, why not go for the **Cowgirl Hall of Fame** on Hudson Street? This is not one of those mass-produced margaritas-from-a-mix "concept restaurants." On the contrary, it's the personal expression of Sherry Delamarter, who is obsessed with things Western, especially cowgirls. There's a little museum in there, and a mock Western living room with a painted night sky above the roof beams; there are glass-

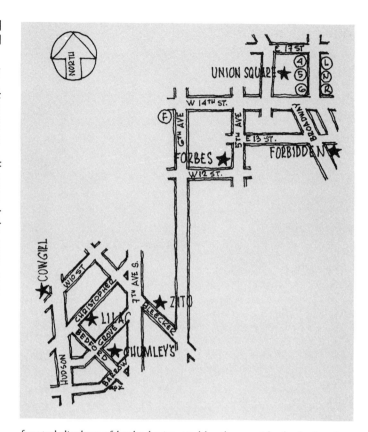

fronted displays of barbed wire, tied by the great barbed-wire tiers of the Old West. This is definitely one woman's vision but wildly appealing to all, as is the Western-cum-Southwestern food and drink. (A special kiddie menu features not just burgers and dogs but also a single cheese enchilada, Frito pie *made in the bag*, and so on.) Everyone here is friendly; on your way out, investigate the campy little gift shop, featuring water-squirting pistols in holsters, beaded belts, bandannas, and cactus salt-and-pepper sets. Then plan to come back sometime for brunch; it's a great menu.

Union Square Greenmarket, Union Square West and 17th St.
Forbidden Planet, 840 Broadway at 13th St. 473-1576
Forbes Magazine Galleries, 62 Fifth Ave. at 12th St. 206-5548
Zito, 259 Bleecker St. bet. Sixth and Seventh Aves. 929-6139

Chumley's Restaurant,

86 Bedford St. bet. Barrow and Grove Sts. 675-4449

Li-Lac Chocolates Inc.,

120 Christopher St. bet. Bleecker and Hudson Sts. 242-7374

Cowgirl Hall of Fame, 519 Hudson St. at 10th St. 633-1133

Getting there: 4, 5, 6, L, N, or R to Union Sq.; F train to 14th St.

* *

Midtown Lite:
Radio City Music Hall's tour,
fancy moviegoing at the Ziegfeld or the Guild,
assorted waterfalls, and an irresistible diner.

Save this trip for a day when you're prepared to spend a bit of
money to get a bit of pampering. The first stop: **Radio City
Music Hall**, for a tour (which you can take any time except
Christmas or Easter). It may
seem corny, but people
do report near-spiri-
tual feelings at the
sight of that gorgeous
place up close and
empty. In the course of 45
minutes, you will study
Radio City's interior architecture, the Mighty Wurlitzer, the prosce-
nium arch, the backstage areas, and the complex workings of the
stage (those big gears and levers are especially thrilling for kids).
Some call it a wonder of the world; you might call it $12 per adult
and $6 per child well spent. Afterwards, wander over to the
Channel Gardens (and the rink to watch the skaters if
it's winter). Show the children as much of Rockefeller Center's
paintings, sculpture, and architectural decoration as they will toler-

ate, and then take the glass-enclosed elevator down from the rink to the lower level. Children will love the ant-colony feel of the bustling concourse, and you will have many choices for food—anything from Mrs. Fields Cookies to Au Bon Pain—and souvenirs (excellent Statues of Liberty made of some green polymer-like substance on a white marble-like base).

The next luxurious stop is a movie, at the **Guild 50th Street Cinema** or the **Ziegfeld Theatre**. This is moviegoing as it used to be—particularly at the Guild, which has thick carpets, soft and comfy seats, the requisite exorbitantly-priced Raisinets etc., and a quiet, anticipatory feel. The Ziegfeld is thrilling in its own gigantic way, with all the Dolby sound and the tall escalators and the blockbuster movies. Either is a far cry from the local multiplex where your feet instantly meld with the gum on the floor and you can hear the movies playing in the theaters on either side.

Next, benign and mellow, check out a couple of **water-falls** on your way west for dinner. The first one, by Isamu Noguchi, is hidden away at 666 Fifth Avenue, in a little alley between 52nd and 53rd streets. Turn a corner and you'll come up against a curtain of water that plays peacefully across aluminum and steel forms in an otherworldly light. Come out blinking and head over to Sixth Avenue, which, just at this point, has spectacular fountains and contemporary sculptures; they provide an excellent counterpoint to the permanent crush of people, cabs, and lunch carts. Head down Sixth to 49th Street and turn west along the side of the McGraw-Hill building. Just behind it, you'll see a little park—investigate and you will find yourself walking through a water tunnel, with (glass-enclosed) water cascading around your head and down beside you.

Finally, dispel whatever feelings of repose this may have engendered with a visit to **Ellen's Star-dust Diner** at 51st Street and Broadway. How to explain this place? It's a fantasy of a fifties diner—all chrome and booths, with a jukebox, TV screens, and waiters in loudly patterned vests. The menu is comfort food of many lands—with everything from fajitas to French fries. Your children will happily chow down on the shakes and malteds, sliders, sandwiches, or chicken potpie. Then there's the little train that goes steadily chugging high up around the perimeter, and, if you can manage to go there after 7 p.m. any night from Wednesday through Saturday, you'll be treated to the sight of singing waitpersons strutting their actor stuff. Oldies on the TV, maybe a lime rickey— and that train. How could you deny your kids this seminal experience?

Radio City Music Hall,
1260 Ave. of the Americas at 50th St. 632-4041
Guild 50th Street Cinema,
33 W. 50th St. bet. Fifth and Sixth Aves. 757-2406
Ziegfeld Theatre,
141 W. 54th St. bet. Sixth and Seventh Aves. 505-CINE #602
Ellen's Stardust Diner, 1650 Broadway at 51st St. 956-5151

Chapter Five

Action without Angst:
You Can All Join In

New York City's wonderful parks: Consider

what you can do: baseball, cricket, field hockey, football, soccer, cro-
quet, bird-watching, basketball, golf, lawn bowling, boccie, rowboat-
ing and canoeing, model-yacht-sailing, nature walks, track and field,
astronomy, paddle ball, cycling,
curling, Rollerblading, fishing,
horseback riding, ice skating, wall
climbing, rock climbing, and swim-
ming. Did we mention softball,
haunted walks and hayrides in season, Buddhist meditations, winter
fairs, equestrian fairs, Highland

games, Easter egg rolls, square dances, yoga classes, chess, checkers,
children's theater and dance? And let's not forget traditional plea-
sures such as feeding the ducks, rolling down hills, and picnicking.
Absolutely the best way to find out what's on is to be in touch with
the Urban Park Rangers. They're courteous and very knowledgable—
and they send out free mailing lists. Like the parks themselves, they
are a resource no parent should ever underestimate. (By the way,
did we leave out free Shakespeare?) Call (800) 201-PARK.

Gateway Sports Center in Brooklyn: You can

reach it by public transportation, but not easily. The trip by car is
worth it, especially if you're a multisport family, as Gateway offers
tennis courts, batting cages with varied levels of pitching speed, a
driving range, and one of the city's prettiest 18-hole miniature golf
courses, with big clumps of pampas grass and a little stream. You
get a great feeling of space out here—it's an open, airy setting, next
to Marine Park and right across from Floyd Bennett Field, once an
army air field famed as Wrong Way Corrigan's point of departure,
now used as a training ground for EMS and police drivers as well as
for occasional events (the most important of which, for our purpos-
es, is the annual Native American Indian Powwow, see page 78).

Just across the causeway is another excellent reason to come out here—the **Gateway National Recreation Area**, a great windswept expanse of marsh and beaches, stretching from Breezy Point to Far Rockaway. **Jacob Riis** beach is the best: it has white sand with large shells, dilapidated WPA-era buildings where you can take a shower or buy something to eat; and a companionable, if well-worn, feel.

> **Gateway Sports Center**, 3200 Flatbush Ave. 718-253-6816

There are **other enticing locales for miniature golf**. One is the **Nellie Bly Amusement Park** in Brooklyn (see page 23) and another is the **Turtle Cove Golf Complex**, located on City Island (this also has batting cages and a driving range). The most elegant little course used to be at Wollman Rink—each of its nine holes was in the shape of a New York landmark. Sadly, the management of the rink has changed and, as of the summer of 1996, the golf is gone.

> **Nellie Bly Amusement Park**, 1824 Shore Pkwy. 718-996-4002
> **Turtle Cove Golf Complex**, 1 City Island Rd., Bx. 718-885-2646

Chelsea Piers: Despite its overwhelming publicity blitz, which would make many cool parents wary, this place can be a nice experience for you and your kids. Sky Rink's two indoor skating rinks are spacious, clean, and light filled, with big windows looking out over the Hudson. Of course, you can sign the children up for all kinds of classes and hockey leagues, but if you just want to give

them something pleasantly active to do for an afternoon, with no strings, you have several options: open basketball games (pay by the hour);

batting cages; the outdoor roller rink; and the driving range (in the golf club), which has kid-size clubs.

Chelsea Piers, 23rd Street and the Hudson River. For Sky Rink, call 336-6100; for children's programs, 336-6666; for the Golf Club, 336-6400; and for general information, 336-6000

Randalls Island:
You know the name, but you've certainly never been there. In fact, where is it exactly? Well, just off the Triborough Bridge, down a road labeled Randalls Island/Downing Stadium. This place is a 400-acre leisure and sports complex, part city owned, part privately owned. The city facilities include tennis courts (permit required), driving range, baseball and soccer fields, and so on, but they are well used, to put it mildly, and somewhat rundown. So head for the Randalls Island Golf and Family Entertainment Center, which has a driving range, two 18-hole miniature golf courses, batting cages (where you can hit softballs, too), and free parking. In the summer, it's open 24 hours a day.

Randalls Island, to find out more call 427-5689

Riverbank:
This is the controversial recreation area built on top of a sewage treatment plant in Harlem. Instead of rejecting it out of hand, why not try it? The reason: it has two Olympic-size pools, one inside and one outdoor, and both of them have a shallow-end depth of four feet. This is, as any parent will know, profoundly reassuring to younger children. It is a clean, new facility, right on the river, with a park for picnicking and skating (Rollerblading year-round and ice skating in the winter); and it's very safe, with both lifeguards and state police on the premises. It's wildly popular, so try and get there early in the day. Take the 1 train to 145th St. and walk one block downhill.

Riverbank, 679 Riverside Dr. 694-3654/3600

Rye Playland: This beautifully maintained, landmarked Art Deco amusement park, with its sturdy old rides, tree-lined walkways, paddleboats on the lake, and tranquil crescent of beach, evokes another, calmer era. The magical boardwalk scenes from Big were filmed here. Playland is fun and clean, and the 45 rides are just exciting enough for all ages. (The roller coaster is downright thrilling.) Why not make an evening trip up here one summer weekend? (On Fridays and Saturdays, it's open late.) To get there, take I-95 north from  Manhattan and turn off at the Playland Parkway. The Metro-North train goes from Grand Central to Rye, where you take a ten-minute ride on the No. 76 bus.

    Rye Playland, to find out more call 914-967-2040

Bird-watching: Because of its strategic location on migratory flight paths, New York is visited seasonally by everything from herons to hawks to weird little warblers, the mere mention of which gets enthusiasts' phone wires humming. At almost any time of year, Urban Park Rangers conduct bird-watching expeditions in parks all over the city. Call (800) 201-PARK to find out more. The real thrill comes in the early spring or fall when masses and masses of birds are on the move. Then, take your young naturalist to **the Ramble in Central Park**, 37 acres of woods and streams that the birds consider a very desirable location (after all, it's Manhattan), and the ***Jamaica Bay Wildlife Refuge***, which is part of the Gateway National Recreation Area (see above). Even if you don't have a car, you can reach this enormous stretch of marsh, dune, and water by subway and foot. Here's how: Put on walking shoes, pack binoculars (and snacks, and a picnic), and take the A train to Far Rockaway. Your stop is Broad

Channel. From the subway, walk one block west to Cross Bay Boulevard and then north three-quarters of a mile to the entrance to the Refuge. (This distance rules out the tinies.) Tours are free, and last up to two hours; there are picnic tables (but no food) and toilets in the Visitors Center.

For *the Ramble* and *all city bird-watching* call (800) 201-PARK

Jamaica Bay Wildlife Refuge, 718-318-4340

Hackers, Hitters, & Hoops:

An indoor sports center for a cold or rainy day, Hackers, Hitters & Hoops is great for those times when youthful high spirits are wreaking havoc on your nerves and infrastructure. This will cost you, because you have to buy tokens to pay for each sport the kids choose; but in the daytime, admission is free, and anyway, the kids' gratitude will more than make up for any needling resentments you might be harboring. In this big, comfy place, you can try billiards, Ping-Pong, air hockey, the "obstacle challenge" (struggling past many puffy vinyl obstructions), virtual reality video games, Twin Peaks (where you can compete against a pal in wall-climbing), and space ball (a ball, a hoop, a trampoline = happiness), as well as the usual suspects (batting cages, basketball, miniature golf, etc.). And the two pinball machines are mesmerizing. At night, the bar opens and corporate America comes in to party; but during the day, however busy the place gets, it's big enough to fully occupy your brood and cozy enough to do it without intimidating them.

Hackers, Hitters, & Hoops, 123 W. 18th St. bet. Sixth and Seventh Aves. 929-7482

South Cove on skates, and, for the littlest ones, the city's best playground: New York abounds in cool places to go **in-line skating**, but one of the coolest has to be along the Hudson River from Chambers Street to South Cove. Here's the plan: Rent your skates from **Alex Sports** on Chambers Street, then head west to the river, and a gloriously eccentric group of animal sculptures by Tom Otterness. Pry the little ones loose from these with the promise of **the city's best playground**, which is a few blocks south, between Vesey and Murray Streets. This state-of-the-art facility is built to delight and, with its chain-link climbing nets, animal-head fountains, and foot-powered red carousel, it succeeds.

All around are benches and grassy lawns for picnics and lazy games of catch, but don't expect the big kids to join you for a while. Not when there's a long esplanade with a special level for cyclists and skaters just waiting to be conquered. Whether experienced on foot or wheels, this place is dreamlike, filled with light, water, and seabirds. As you pass the World Financial Center and keep going south, the artiness gets more prevalent, with elaborate plantings and vaguely nautical sculptural installations much in evidence. South Cove itself is probably the most atmospheric stretch of waterfront in the city, with its boulders, tall grasses, wooden pilings, cobalt-blue lanterns, and Japanese bridges. You'll want to come back often. And by late 1996 or 1997, you'll be able to go right round the island's tip, all the way to the Battery.

For **Hudson River Park** playground and special events information (kite-making, fishing, etc.), call Battery Park City Park Corporation at 267-9700

Alex Sports, 295 Greenwich St. north of Chambers St. 964-1944

action without angst: you can all join in / 111

Chapter Six

Pay for Play: Ten Treats that are Fun for Kids, Easy for Parents

1. *Playspace, Discovery Zone, Wondercamp*

Playspace is gentle, creative, and pitched to the younger set (dress-up, sand, splashing); **Discovery Zone** is exhausting, loud, and pricey (once the little ones discover the arcade games); **Wondercamp** is labyrinthine and exhaustive (from computer games to ballet classes). What they have in common: you can leave the children to hurtle (safely) around every nook and cranny while you sit with coffee and the paper.

Playspace, 2473 Broadway at 92nd St. 769-2300, and 1504 Third Ave at 85th St. 717-5200

Discovery Zone, (Manhattan) 258-278 Eighth Ave at 23rd St. 691-6610; (Brooklyn) 5405 Kings Plaza 718-252-1717 and the Gallery at Metrotech 718-694-9600; (Queens) Metro Mall Shopping Center, 6626 Metropolitan Ave. and Middle Village 718-821-2533; (Staten Island) Pergament Shopping Center, 2795 Richmond Ave. 718-370-0400; (Bronx) 237 East Fordham Rd. 718-329-5437

Wondercamp, 27 W.23rd St. bet. Fifth and Sixth Aves. 243-1111

2. *Pull Cart Ceramics*

Seven floors up in a Flatiron District loft, ceramic mugs, bowls, and vases are displayed unadorned. Your child gets to pick one and make it beautiful. There are people to advise and booklets with visual suggestions. After you're done, leave the artwork there for a week to be fired and glazed. Price: $6 an hour, plus the cost of the item chosen.

Pull Cart Ceramics, 31 W. 21st St. bet. Fifth and Sixth Aves. 727-7089

3. *The Museum of Television & Radio*

Look, nobody's perfect. It's OK, really, if sometimes you want to just sit placidly with your kids and stare at reruns of old TV shows. Call them "classic" if it makes you feel better. And at the high-tech Museum of Television & Radio they do have classics, everything

from "The Ed Sullivan Show" (hey, wanna see the Beatles' first appearance?) to "The Lone Ranger" and "I Love Lucy." You can call up four selections on the computer and then watch them on a console for up to two hours.

The Museum of Television & Radio, 25 W. 52nd St. bet. Fifth and Sixth Aves. 621-6600 or 621-6800 for tape. Call for details and to find out about special showings for children.

4. Baubles, Bangles, Bargains

Take your budding Mizrahi or Karan notion shopping at the Cinderella Flower and Feather Co. (60 W. 38th St. bet. Fifth and Sixth Aves. 840-0644), the Fabric Warehouse (406 Broadway), and Gampel Supply for beads and such (39 W. 37th St. bet. Fifth and Sixth Aves. 398-9222). And, as a weekend way of life, take them to your local flea market, where some will rummage among the ancient purses, vests, or posters while others can pick up a tiny tank or old comic for $1. They're New Yorkers, after all, so they must learn these things.

5. Crafts on Broadway, Little Shop of Plaster

Both of these places offer children ages three and up (but it would be smart to wait until they're at least four and have the requisite dexterity to make something truly spiffy-looking) the chance to do some plaster craft, which means that they select a ready-made plaster mold from hundreds on display, then decorate it with paint, and glitter or finger-wax it. The finished masterpiece is glazed on the premises, to be taken home then and there. Prices start at about $10. Sand art and T-shirt painting are also available, and at Crafts on Broadway you can buy many kinds of supplies, including fancy stationery.

Crafts on Broadway, 215 W. 76th St. bet. Broadway and Amsterdam Aves. 501-7320

Little Shop of Plaster, 106 W. 90th St. bet. Columbus and Amsterdam Aves. 877-9771; and 431 E. 73rd St. bet. 1st and York Aves. 717-6636

6. The Petrel

She's only 70 feet long, but she's fast and beautiful and she sails around the Harbor or up the Hudson from Battery Park, May through September. This is not the Circle Line, this is actual sailing (without having to do any of the work). For details call: 825-1976.

7. Tea at the Plaza Hotel

Go only if your daughter is absolutely obsessed with *Eloise*, that wonderful book about a spirited little girl who lives and runs wild in the hotel. Why only then? Because it costs $22 per person. For that, you sit in the Palm Court, nibbling little sandwiches, scones and pastries, tea and coffee (and maybe your request for a soda will be indulged), accompanied by the tasteful sounds of a pianist and violinist. If all this sounds enticing, see if you can dig out that nice flowered dress and a pair of shiny Mary Janes for her, some discreet pearls for Mom, and get on over there.

The Plaza Hotel is at 768 Fifth Ave. at Central Park S. 759-3000

8. The Bead Store

Your child (presumably, but not necessarily your daughter) can pick from a stunning selection of beads and design a necklace on a

round tray. There's help with stringing if needed, and the necklaces are finished off for free. With beads individually priced, the necklaces end up costing anywhere from $5 to $25 or $30. Pretty good, considering that you yourself do not have to tie any knots.

The Bead Store, 1065 Lexington Ave. bet. 75th and 76th Sts. 628-4383; and 132 Spring St. bet. Greene and Wooster Sts. 941-6450

9. Tram to Roosevelt Island and back, followed by Serendipity 3

You've gone by it and speculated about it. What are you waiting for? The tram departs from Second Avenue and 60th Street every 15 minutes, and at the other end you're in a quiet little place that's so unlike the city, you feel it doesn't deserve its 212 area code. The excitingly ruined hospitals and asylums are, alas, all fenced off; so walk north and find an open space for sitting or picnicking or one of the numerous playgrounds for your youngest. Then, back on the tram, and make straight for the campy, eccentric charm of Serendipity 3, to remind yourself what New York is all about. Sit elbow-to-elbow with movie stars and their kids, tourists, and birthday celebrants. Go for the dishes that have stood the test of time: the foot-long hot dogs, frozen hot chocolate, and the divine Miss Milton's lovely fudge pie. Go crazy and buy a T-shirt, too.

Roosevelt Island Tramway, 832-4543

Serendipity 3, 225 E. 60th St. bet. Second and Third Aves. 838-3531

10. Barnes & Noble

Not only are these stores all over town, they're well-disposed towards children. Storytimes, pajama party-storytimes, author appearances, and special events abound. Go to one of the trendy new stores, buy lots of pretty paperbacks, and then slump companionably over muffins in the cafe—if you can get in without tripping over all the strollers, that is.

Chapter Seven

Downtime: Ten all-time great New York movies that you will be able to watch happily, at least for the first few times, with your kids

NOTE: As of this writing, all of these films are available on video. Some of them (i.e. *Searching for Bobby Fischer*) may be over the heads of smaller children. Then again, maybe not. As cool parents, you know what is or isn't appropriate fare for your family.

1. *The World of Henry Orient:* A Brooklyn con artist turned foreign-born concert pianist and the two preadolescent girls who worship him. Peter Sellers is inspired as Henry, Tippy Walker is delightful as the more troubled of two girls, and Angela Lansbury is an excellent villainess. Central Park in winter has never looked lovelier.

2. *Superman:* Christopher Reeves's bow as the legend refurbished for the big screen. Farewell baggy tights and dopey flying effects, hello Margot Kidder and a raft of terrific character actors, including Gene Hackman and Valerie Perrine, whose hideout is located in the bowels of Grand Central Station.

3. *Tootsie:* Dustin Hoffman's finest hour as a starving actor who becomes a soap opera diva. As sweet as it is hilarious, this gender-bender also features fine contributions from Bill Murray, Terri Garr, Jessica Lange, Dabney Coleman, and Charles Durning.

4. King Kong: The world's most soulful ape has dignity even when hanging off the Empire State Building. And Fay Wray can really scream! Has a special relevance in these days of kids' bath soap in shapes of endangered species.

5. Guys and Dolls: Frank before sainthood, Marlon before statehood, Times Square before porn or gentrification. Purists may carp that Marlon's playing Frank's role and can't sing, but it still has the finest score of all American musicals, along with a wonderful supporting cast (Viva Vivian Blaine and Stubby Kaye!), great sets and costumes, and foist-class Noo Yawk accents.

6. West Side Story: If only juvenile delinquency were really this way. This urban Romeo and Juliet has the power to squeeze tears from anyone old enough to follow the plot—recommended for ten and up. The exteriors were shot where Lincoln Center stands today.

7. Searching for Bobby Fischer: Based on a true story, this movie about an American chess prodigy who gets his start among the patzers of Washington Square makes the ancient game seem as cool as hoops.

8. Miracle on 34th Street: Santa Claus comes to town and finds it full of skeptics. This Christmas fable tempers its sentimentality with a nice dose of city wit, but cool parents and kids alike will melt as Edmund Gwenn makes everyone's Chistmas dreams come true. Younger children will fade during some of the romantic longuers. Catch the shots of Macy's Thankgiving Day Parade before television, commercialism, and balloon technology transformed it; here, it might as well be a small-town parade. Even though this is shown endlessly on TV during the holidays, rent it; it's much, much better without commercials. And make sure it's the 1947 original, not the appalling remake with Richard Attenborough.

9. *On the Town:* The patter's a little sluggish and the musical numbers overlong by today's standards, but the opening ("New York, New York") is heaven, the location shots of Manhattan in the fifties are fascinating (catch Columbus Circle pre-Coliseum). As for Frank, Gene, Ann (Miller), Betty (Garrett), and Jules (Munshin)—they're a helluva cast.

10. *A Tree Grows in Brooklyn:* Elia Kazan's first film displays his always extraordinary work with actors. A four-hankie weeper set in Williamsburg, Brooklyn, around the turn of the century, this story of a loving family and its tribulations is best for older children, who will love the views of children at play in a bygone New York (especially the Christmas tree scene). The brilliant child actress Peggy Ann Garner will steal your heart.

Honorable mention: The **Ghostbusters** may be too scary for the tinies, but they've got raucous New York atmosphere, slimed landmarks, and a walking Statue of Liberty.

Chapter Eight

Ten Places to Visit and Things to Do for Which No Parent Should Ever Be Too Cool

1. Don't be too cool to join the tourists at the Radio City Music Hall Christmas Show.

Why? Because it's there. Despite its maudlin religiosity, the $5 mega-Cokes, and the incessant drone of outlanders, this show really is the last of its kind—a gaudy spectacle of wooden soldiers, live animals, religious tableaux, and the resonant blast of the mighty Wurlitzer. If you should be fortunate enough to witness a live camel obeying the call of nature during the incredibly discreet manger scene, your children will be grateful to you forever. For you, there are the Rockettes, still alive and kicking. Afterwards, zip around the corner and take in the skyscraping Rockefeller Center Christmas tree, another classic, astounding New York sight left too long to the tourists.

Radio City Music Hall Christmas Spectacular, call 247-4777

2. Don't be too cool to ride on a carousel.

Carousels are one of the few rides children and their parents can sincerely enjoy together. They're safe and easy, they make everyone smile, and they go surprisingly fast; so you should never pass up a chance to climb onto one. Central Park's (65th Street at mid-park, 879-0244) is often so full of courting couples and sensitive singles, you'd think children weren't allowed on, but they are. Prospect Park's (just south of the zoo, 718-965-8999) is a showcase for the restorers who've brought it back. There are two in Queens, one of them in Flushing Meadows at 111th Street and 54th Avenue (718-592-6539), another in Forest Park at Woodhaven Boulevard and Park Lane (718-805-5572). And don't forget the B&B in Coney Island (see page 86); it's enclosed and a little dingy, but it has a real brass ring to grab for.

3. Don't be too cool to take a round-trip ride on the Staten Island Ferry.

Sure, it's a cliché, and it was more fun when you could drive on, and it used to cost a nickel. Still, the Staten Island Ferry (foot of Whitehall Street next to Battery Park; 718-815-BOAT) offers one of the only world-class bargains to which New York can still lay claim. Every half hour or so (call for schedules), a ferry pulls away from its docking bay; half an hour or so later, it reaches its destination. Along the way, you've smelled the sea and felt its spray, cruised right by the Statue of Liberty, and experienced no seasickness. The boats themselves look old, battered and wonderful, with vintage linoleum in patterns that haven't been made for in 30 years and wooden benches worn dark and smooth. The food is nothing special, but the hot dogs taste absolutely wonderful at sea, with breezes blowing and engines churning loudly in the background. In fact, munching as you gaze at the Manhattan skyline or Lady Liberty, you'll swear they're the best hot dogs you've ever had in your life.

4. Don't be too cool to experience the Bronx Zoo (except that now it's the International Wildlife Conservation Park).

Don't make the mistake of bringing the kids here when they're too young to appreciate it. All too often Dad ends up with someone on his shoulders who doesn't give a damn about the life-cycle of the slow loris. How old is old enough for the zoo? A word to the wise: Don't go until your kids are so big they'd be embarrassed to have

you carry them. At that age, they can enjoy the World of Darkness with its swooping bats, glittering-eye lemurs and bush babies, and, weirdest of all, the subterranean colony of naked mole rats. They can take the Bengali Express monorail and see the wild animals they've dreamed of—elephants, tigers, rhinos. They'll love the African plains with their lions, cheetahs, and zebras. For children weary of New York's other "Wildlife Centers," where prairie dogs and sheep and otters stand in for big game, this is the real thing. The Bronx Zoo is like no other zoo in the world. **The International Wildlife Conservation Park**, Fordham Rd./Bronx River Parkway 718-220-5100

5. Don't be too cool to visit the American Museum of Natural History.

True, all too often the revamped dinosaur collection is a mob scene too ghastly to contemplate, but not to worry, there are plenty of other attractions:

* Remember Holden Caulfield and his rapt classmates peering down the bodice of the squaw in the glass case? Well, the figures and tableaux of prehistoric and aboriginal peoples (some naked) are irresistible to young viewers.

* The Hall of Minerals sounds musty, but it's not, not with an actual hunk of moon rock on show and meteors you can touch.

* The huge blue whale, hanging from the ceiling as graceful and lowering as a storm cloud, is astounding. Little children

can spin and race around the polished floor beneath it while you sit and eat something—or maybe even treat yourselves to a drink! (There's a bar there.)

* The museum's ground floor cafeteria is less expensive than the tonier Garden Cafe and resembles a thoroughly unexceptional fast food joint. It is, however, operated by Restaurant Associates, a high-end food service, and the food is much better than you expect it to be. The burgers, in fact, are downright juicy.

American Museum of Natural History, Central Park at W. 79th St. 769-5100

6. Don't be too cool to go to the top of the Empire State Building.

Probably you went up it as a child. It's time to go again, soon, and make it a habit. Try going at dusk or on a summer night, or even on a foggy day when the tips of the surrounding buildings poke through the cottony cloud cover. It's just scary enough for the kids to realize how high up they are; the mere fact of taking three elevators up to the top is impressive. Unfortunately, the wonderfully odd and decrepit Guinness World Records Exhibit Hall (the museum that time forgot) has closed down. Don't try to compensate for this loss by taking the Skyride, a jolting, 25-minute "big-screen flight simulator" tour of New York. It will make your younger children queasy and give you the feeling that you've been had.

   P.S. Before leaving, linger in the entrance lobby for the wonderful relief image of the building on the wall, and especially for the (newly cleaned up) diorama of King Kong, camera in hand, climbing the tower.

For details call: 736-3100

7. Don't be too cool to climb all the stairs to the top of the Statue of Liberty.

It's worth the small inconveniences—tourists of many lands milling about hopelessly, sweltering heat, long lines, etc.—to see the Statue of Liberty. Just allow a lot of time and take bottled water and sunhats if it's summer (waiting for the boat can be a pitiless process). Or else be bold and make the trip off-season. (Choose Saturday over Sunday; the lines won't be so long.) Once there, trek all 354 steps to the top. It takes a while, and you should be prepared for some vertiginous moments as you get close to the crown and you're wedged together with all the other climbers on the vertical plane. (So you should save this trip until you feel your children can handle it without getting trembly.) It's mysterious, thrilling, and awesome to be inside that dark, cavernous exoskeleton—especially if you go on a thundery day when the lights flicker and you can see the lightning play over the skyline. The gift shop is a must —you'll be giggly and lightheaded enough after your adventure to pose for pics in those dopey green foam-rubber crowns.

Take the Circle Line-Statue of Liberty Ferry from the Battery, 269-5755. For hours of operation and prices call Liberty Island, 363-3200. **NOTE:** Your ferry ticket to the Lady includes passage to Ellis Island, which is newly refurbished and profoundly affecting. Its impact, however, depends on understanding what went on there; so we strongly recommend that you take your children there only when they are old enough—third-graders at least—to know something of the island's history and its meaning to Americans.

8. Don't be too cool to go bowling.

Time was when bowling was the fastest-growing family sport in the U.S., and bowling alleys sprouted all over the city the way micro-breweries do today. Those days are gone. Only two bowling alleys now remain in Manhattan, and they're called "lanes," or better yet, "bowling centers." Bowlmor, in Greenwich Village, lacks the all-important, gutter-closing bumpers that are essential for children. The **Leisure Time Bowling and Recreation Center**, a 30-lane facility at the Port Authority Bus Terminal, has gutter guards, a small arcade with air hockey and spiffy video games, plenty of fast food and drinks, leagues of all sorts and the occasional celebrity bowling event.

Outside Manhattan, bowling venues are all around. For our money, the **Gil Hodges Lanes** in far-off Marine Park, Brooklyn, is a treat worth the trip: a spacious, state-of-the-art establishment whose gutter-blockers appear at the yank of a lever by one of the lads who operate the joint. There are 64 lanes, baseball memorabilia on the walls (Gil Hodges himself founded this establishment), a centrally located bar next to a well-lit and perfectly decent food service (nachos, fries and dogs are the order of the day). Parking is a cinch; there's a lot. Or take the D train to Avenue U, then the B3 bus to Mill Avenue; turn right, walk one block, turn right again on Strickland, and there you are. Bring something to read during the trip, and possibly some snacks, games, old New Yorkers, etc.

Leisure Time Bowling and Recreation Center, 625 Eighth Ave. (at Port Authority Bus Terminal) 268-6909

Gil Hodges Lanes, 6161 Strickland Ave., Brooklyn 718-763-3333

9. Don't be too cool to go on a day trip to the beach.

The city beaches are funky, let's face it. Even at Jacob Riis beach, which is the best maintained, you'll find yourself at awfully close quarters with other people's music, children, and private lives. So get up very early one day and take yourselves off to Jones Beach. It, too can be crowded; but it's a state park, with dunes, surf, and miles and miles of beach. It's an easy trip from Penn Station, and all you have to do once you arrive at Jones Beach Station is trot down the stairs and into the bus. In ten minutes or so, you'll have sand between your toes. There are optimistic buildings from the thirties; there's everything you need in terms of food, drink, and bathrooms. Remember, early is definitely best here; so that by the time the crowds are heaviest and the sun is at its most relentless, you'll be ready for home. The number of Jones Beach State Park is 516-785-1600. For train schedules and prices, call the Long Island Railroad at 718-217-5477.

10. Don't be too cool to take that long-postponed trip to the Liberty Science Center.

True, the Liberty Science Center is Over the Big Water in New Jersey. So what? The Cool Parents' tent is a big tent. And this place is close, an airy, spacious setting, both indoors and out, with killer views of the skyline and the harbor, and so many kid-friendly (and even adult-painless) things to see and do that it's worth a family trip.

A caveat for the first-time visitor: Liberty Science Center is so close to the city via road (under ten miles: just through the Holland Tunnel, keep to the right, go a few yards on the Turnpike, and voila!) that you may foolishly think you can drive there in a flash. NOT NECESSARILY. It's quite likely that you will sit in endless, tedious, soul-destroying traffic in the tunnel, where the light is depressing, the air is foul, and you can't get any radio reception (if you must drive, bring

tapes). In no time you'll be wondering where everything started to go wrong in your life and the children will be getting carsick. If you find this prospect daunting, and you should, grab the ferry from downtown Manhattan (see below).

Once arrived, you have decisions to make. Should you start with the IMAX movie and the other presentations? Our recommendation: Do the exhibits first and save the movies for when the kids run out of steam.

There's something for all ages here. Start at the top, where toddlers can get involved in structured play on environmental themes in an area called The Greenhouse, while their older siblings struggle across the climbing wall or squirm through the Touch Tunnel. Everybody will get a kick out of the computerized door frame, which tells you your height when you stand in it (and then tells you to move along), the cutaway worm farm, and the exotic insects, if that's what you call these amazingly hefty creatures: millipedes the size of snakes, Giant Prickly Stick Insects that look like moving branches, Central American cave cockroaches that will make you grateful you don't hang out in Central American caves, and, of course, an enormous, brown, furry tarantula. Eeeewwww. Decompress in the Estuary/Atmosphere area, where the warty sea robin tooling around in its tank is as scary as it gets.

You probably won't spend much time on the health floor, which features an actual ambulance, but is otherwise something of a snooze. The inventions and wizardry downstairs are really fun, though. There's virtual basketball, which pits volunteers from the

audience against computer-generated opponents; a "perception maze" full of fun house mirrors and optical illusions; a Formula One car; and myriad flashy tricks that everyone can do. Don't miss the liquid nitrogen demonstration; the frozen balloons and rubber balls go over big.

The Laser Light Cafe serves basic fast food as well as (bless the LSC's heart) beer and wine. It's okay, and it's also the only game in town. The gift shop is huge and features the usual inventory, in greater array than anywhere except possibly the American Museum of Natural History (which, after all, has two gift shops). In addition to the usual yucky astronaut ice-cream, connecting toys, and bits of semiprecious stone, you'll find ready-to-assemble models of human lungs and other body parts, as well as skull-shaped maracas and the once-rare-but-fast-becoming-as-common-as-dirt punching skeleton puppets. What is the Liberty Science Center doing selling skull-shaped maracas? It's exactly the kind of thing you'll worry about if you have to drive back in traffic.

The Liberty Science Center is located in Liberty State Park, at exit 14B off the New Jersey Turnpike. Call 201-200-1000 for information. To get there without a car, on weekends take a ferry from the World Financial Center to Liberty State Park and a free shuttle bus from there. On weekdays, the ferry goes from the World Financial Center to Colgate Center in Jersey City, from which you take the 31 bus. For ferries, call NY Waterway at 1-800-53-FERRY; for buses, 201-432-8046. In the summer, you can also take an express bus straight there from the Port Authority Bus Terminal at Eighth Ave. and 40th St. Call Academy Bus Lines at 971-9054 for details.

Notes

About the Authors

Between them, Alfred Gingold and Helen Rogan have published six books, including *Items from Our Catalog* (Gingold) and *Mixed Company: Women in the Modern Army* (Rogan). They've written for *New York Woman, The New York Times, Life, Time,* and many other publications. They live in Brooklyn with their son.